East from the Andes

Pioneer Settlements
in the South American Heartland

Raymond E. Crist
Charles M. Nissly

University of Florida Press / Gainesville / 1973

EDITORIAL COMMITTEE
Social Sciences Monographs

Library of Congress Cataloging in Publication Data

Crist, Raymond E.   1904–
    East from the Andes; *see slip*
    (University of Florida social sciences monograph no. 50)
    Bibliography: p. 165-166.
    1. Land settlement—Venezuela. 2. Land settlement—Bolivia. 3. Migration, Internal—South America.
I. Nissly, Charles M., 1934–   joint author.
II. Title. III. Series: Florida. University,
Gainesville. University of Florida monographs. Social sciences, no. 50.
HD576.C74   333.3′23′098   73–10052
ISBN 0–8130–0395–4

PRINTED BY THE STORTER PRINTING COMPANY
GAINESVILLE, FLORIDA

Preface

This study is an endeavor to gather into one volume the material dealing with human penetration and settlement of Andean borderlands between Venezuela and Bolivia. The chapters on Venezuela and Colombia are excerpts from earlier papers by the senior author that have been edited, augmented, and updated. These papers appeared in *The Geographical Review* and *The Annual Report of the Smithsonian Institution* and are excerpted with permission.

This is not merely a chronicle of settlement, but a discussion of the cultural, sociohistorical, and economic factors of settlement, together with their interrelationships *in time* set against the physical backdrop of tropical landscapes. In a work of this kind, extending over many years, much thought has been given to, and reading done in, possibilities of worldwide settlement and the philosophy of peasants.

The senior author has for several decades carried out studies of the influence of land tenure systems on land management practices in many parts of the world. This background has proved helpful in the analysis of data on de jure and de facto systems of land tenure and their influence on land use practices in the South American tropics.

In this volume, studies are made of human migration into the hot, humid areas to the south and east, for the most part, of the great Andean chain. To understand better the phenomenon of immigration, one should first survey the minds and souls of those people who are leaving the Andes. Whether community Indians, self-sufficient mestizo farmers, or herdsmen of llamas and alpacas on the high, bleak plateaus, they are men without hope of ever bettering their lot in their place of birth. They are tired of the repression and violence of the landlords, of the gulf that separates them from the overlords, even from the urban elite and tiny middle class. They have come to hate their position as serfs in a society where hunger, misery, and unbelievable poverty are the only rewards for lifetimes of unremitting toil, in which the level of living achieved is only barely consistent with the survival of the human species.

Roads for wheeled vehicles are rapidly replacing the trails that for centuries tied mountain villages to the outside world, trodden only by the bare feet of human beings or the hooves of pack animals. Such roads, with their jeeps, cars, and trucks, represent a kind of safety hatch for those who will and can leave the Middle Ages, either for the twentieth-century life in towns or cities or for the unpopulated stretches to the east. The uninhabited sections of the Amazon and Orinoco basins were once avoided because of the health dangers, but with roads comes an awareness of modern public health practices. Living in the tropics is no longer synonymous with an early death. The rain forest is no longer considered the enemy, but rather a haven for those with a will to work.

The senior author first went to Venezuela as a geologist in 1928–31. He worked along the mountain front of the Venezuelan Andes between Acarigua and San Antonio de Caparo. His immediate chief, Mr. Rolf Engleman, as well as other officers of the Atlantic Refining Company, were extremely cooperative in making maps, photographs, and field notes available. Field observations were organized in the paper "Along the Llanos-Andes Border in Zamora, Venezuela," and these observations, supplemented with library material, formed the basis of his dissertation in geography at the University of Grenoble, under the late Professor Raoul Blanchard.

In 1940 the John Simon Guggenheim Memorial Foundation made possible fifteen months in the field, during which time he was able to study many aspects of human geography between Venezuela and Bolivia, in the high mountains as well as along the eastern piedmont belt.

In 1944, under the auspices of the Rubber Development Corporation of the United States government, he was able to intensify his studies in eastern Bolivia, and in 1949, as cultural geographer with the Institute of Social Anthropology of the Smithsonian Institution, he cooperated with the Director of the Instituto Etnológico of the Universidad del Cauca in Popayán, Colombia, in intensive studies and broad reconnaissance surveys of land tenure systems and modern-day land use practices.

He worked closely with a number of outstanding Colombian ar-
chaeologists and anthropologists and visited the great monuments
of San Agustin; he came to appreciate the importance of studying
the long evolution of man's incumbency on the earth if one were
to understand the present-day patterns of land use, human occupance, and cultural diversity, and if one were to plan for possible
changes in the future.

He has investigated scores of settlements already made or in process of formation in the belt to the east of the great Andean chain.
He has kept an open mind as to the influences of the physical and
cultural factors that spelled success or failure, or bare survival, for
these settlements. Thousands of items in his field notes were di-
gested, hopefully in accord with the observation of Santayana: "The
traveller should be an artist recomposing what he sees; then he can
carry away the picture and add it to a transmissible fund of wisdom,
not as further miscellaneous experience but as a corrected view of
the truth" (*My Host the World*, vol. 3, *Of Persons and Places* [New
York: Charles Scribner's Sons, 1953], p. 35).

In 1954, under a special or continuing grant of the John Simon
Guggenheim Memorial Foundation, he began systematically, summer after summer, to go back and forth from the Andes to the
eastern hot country, collecting information and observations on
migration and settlement and the cultural and the physical factors
operative in favoring or impeding them. More recently, continued
field investigations in the eastern Andes have been carried out
under a generous grant of the Agricultural Development Corporation, which also provided expenses for training in field methods
for graduate students at the University of Florida.

In the course of this work, he has come into intimate contact with
the rural people of Andean borderlands who live out their all too
short, seemingly obscure lives dependent upon the earth under their
feet and upon the heavens above, living by the rhythms and im-
mutable rules laid down by the imperatives of sun and soil and
rain. They toil and struggle with their bare hands and a single cutting tool to wrest a living from a nature so bountiful in many things
other than human foodstuffs. They greet the stranger with the
quiet, innate dignity that is the birthright of those who feel be-
holden to no one; they are eager of speech, especially when con-
versation is about their children, their crops, the weather. Many
are keen of mind, with glowing bright eyes, even when their bodies

are gaunt and lean from hard work and irregular, inadequate meals. They are not educated in the formal sense, but they are superb human beings, intelligent, warm of heart, hospitable to a fault. They pass on the spark of life because they are a hardy breed with great vitality, with a monumental force, an unquenchable will to live; they are the descendants of those who have for centuries survived precarious, marginal existences.

We have tried to give significant facets of the history of migration into, and settlement of, Andean borderlands. Later information from researchers currently working in the field will help fill the gaps in this volume as well as the gaps on the map of the heartland of South America.

The junior author first became interested in life in the tropical rain forest during the summer of 1959 when he lived in a Shipibo Indian village in eastern Peru; later, he journeyed down the Amazon River. Subsequently, he spent a year investigating the opening up of Brazil's Far West for his doctoral dissertation at the University of Florida. Work in Colombia and Venezuela further spurred his interest in tropical lowland settlement possibilities in Andean America.

Both senior and junior authors have observed that where man has wooed the physical landscape for centuries, as for example in the Far East, in northwestern Europe, and along the Mediterranean, a modus vivendi has been achieved between man and his environment. In contrast, some of the most bedraggled and depleted landscapes are to be found in areas newly settled during the last century, or even during the last decade. This is especially true of the vast sector of the hot, humid tropics under study. Observations in the field of the settlement process in its divers aspects and facets have been made; tens of thousands of acres of forest land are being cleared annually for cropland and pastureland; the physical and cultural factors that have helped spell success or failure of these settlement activities have been analyzed.

Certain consequences of deforestation in tropical forest lands are obvious, such as the great waste of wood and lumber products and the rapid runoff and erosion on steep slopes, just as they were when the woodlands of the United States were being destroyed. (There was no one to tell the settler in southern Ohio in 1870 not to clear a beech wood in order to make a cornfield, and if there had been he would have paid no attention. Indeed, his descendants are still doing the same thing in 1970!) At present we simply do not know what will be the long-range and overall effects of deforestation in the tropical rain forests of the Americas. The authors would consider it an act of prudence to give high priority to basic research—carried out *in the tropics*—in climatology, soil science, botany, and animal husbandry. Human adaptation of areas in the hot humid tropics of Africa and Asia, which has been going on for millenia, might provide certain guidelines for those who are investigating the same phenomenon in the tropics of the New World. In the next few years basic information will become available on the effects on the ecology of the Transamazonian Highway, now being constructed across Brazil, the last great land frontier zone on earth; perhaps definitive works can then be written on that subject. Meanwhile, without passing judgment, significant aspects of the history of migration into lowlands and of the settlement and colonization of humid tropical Andean borderlands will be discussed.

René Dubos, an internationally known humanist in the environmental movement, points out the danger of emphasizing only the destructive aspects of man's impact on his environment; he urges that we cultivate positive environmental values, for "many of the Earth's potentialities remained unexpressed until they were brought out by human labor, imagination and, indeed, fantasy" ("How Man Helps Nature," in *Smithsonian*, December 1972, p. 20). Many classic landscapes, from the foggy, windswept Scottish moors to the sun-drenched Mediterranean, illustrate the fact that the human quality of the environment may transcend physical and ecological considerations; what we see in those countries now is a man-made, not a natural milieu; harmony with nature has been attained through intelligent dealings with it.

As Dubos concludes in "How Man Helps Nature," "we can manipulate the raw stuff of nature to shape it into environments which are ecologically sound, economically profitable, esthetically rewarding and favorable to the growth of the human spirit" (p. 28).

We gratefully acknowledge the assistance of the Center for Latin American Studies in providing a cartographer and typist as well as a reader who gave the manuscript a constructively critical reading. Thanks must go also to the Graduate School of the University of Florida for making possible the publication of this monograph.

In a work of this scope, place names and foreign terms are used extensively. Therefore, to avoid the repetitious use of "see map," most place names encountered in the text can be located on the maps which accompany the chapters on Venezuela, Colombia, Ecuador, Peru, and Bolivia. Foreign terms are italicized only the first time they are used in each chapter. Chapters 2–6 have bibliographies pertaining to particular countries, and there is a general bibliography at the end of the book.

Contents

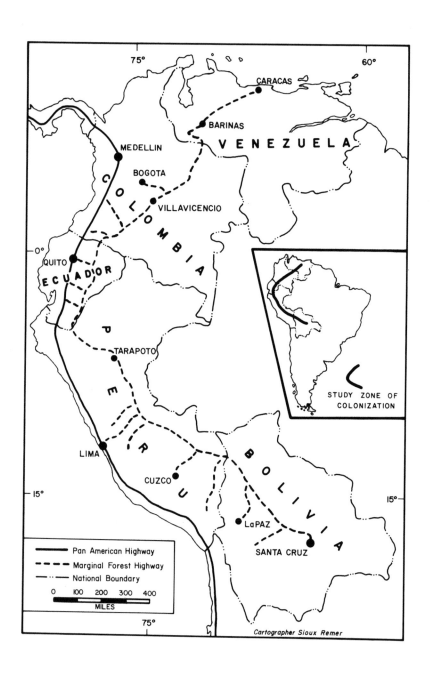

CARACAS

BARINAS

V E N E Z U E L A

MEDELLIN

BOGOTA

VILLAVICENCIO

C
O
L
O
M
B
I
A

QUITO

E C U A D O R

P
E
R
U

TARAPOTO

LIMA

CUZCO

B
O
L
I
V
I
A

LaPAZ

SANTA CRUZ

STUDY ZONE OF
COLONIZATION

——— Pan American Highway
‑ ‑ ‑ Marginal Forest Highway
‑·‑·‑ National Boundary

0   100   200   300   400
MILES

75°

Cartographer Sioux Remer

75°   60°

0°

15°   15°

1. Prologue

THE GREAT MASS of the rural proletariat of Andean America has always lived a marginal existence, economically, politically, and socially. The core and continuum of their lives have been poverty. Although they are economically, socially, and even culturally deprived peoples, they have survived. Their "scarcity economy," or "poverty mentality," or "culture of poverty"—the term given currency by Oscar Lewis—or whatever name one pleases to give it, must have had real survival value, for the carriers of that culture are here today, very much alive, if not exactly thriving, in this last third of the twentieth century. In their desperate struggle for the minimal amount of the food and shelter consonant with their survival, these Andean peasants have been prey to the envy, distrust, deceit, vicious gossip, lies, and, not infrequently, the physical violence of their fellows. But they have survived.

The economic outlook of the Andean peasantry is probably well summed up in the story of the farmer who, when asked if he had received the price he had expected for his hogs that spring, replied: "No, but then I didn't expect to." And no wonder. Harvests are getting more and more meager as soil fertility wanes, and the soil washes away, and pest problems become more acute. Technology is archaic. Illiteracy is the rule, and folk methods rather than modern science are depended on as guides in farming. Ill health, malnutrition, and desperate, crushing poverty have conditioned the population to attitudes of hopelessness, resignation, and fatalism. The circle of life and hope has been so small and so tight that it has been impossible for the individual to escape from the immemorial way of life, or even to think of wanting to escape.

Each peasant has been born into a world of poverty, has known nothing else all his life, and will bequeath to his children as his only legacy the traditions of poverty. A removal of the barriers to

1

economic development is not always enough; as Oscar Lewis has suggested, the culture of poverty may be more difficult to eliminate in some areas than poverty itself, for certain patterns of life, non-economic life goals, have been perpetuated over generations and they are not going to be changed easily. No man is an island. As Foster so perceptively writes, "In the traditional peasant society hard work and thrift are moral qualities of only the slightest functional value. Given the limitations of land and technology, additional hard work in village productive enterprises simply does not produce a significant increment in income. It is pointless to talk of thrift in a subsistence economy in which most producers are at the economic margin; there is usually nothing to be thrifty about."[1]

Social and Cultural Controls

The wealthy elite.—The rich and the powerful, the dominant class, wish to preserve the status quo of the Andean peasantry; they tend to explain away low economic status as being the result of personal inferiority and inadequacy. But the peasants are aware that the dominant people in society neither toil nor spin, that they were born as owners of land and wealth, able to manipulate those controls and sanctions which the police, priests, teachers, and government officials are able to impose. Peasants know that the powerful do not prize thrift simply because they do not have to—they have their property and wealth, hence they do not have to accumulate it. They can literally afford the "caballero" or "gentleman" complex, feeling superior to those who have to work with their hands and walk to market with their produce. They can indulge in conspicuous consumption and waste by buying Parisian gowns, cream-colored Cadillacs, and walled-in, nonfunctional homes because they have the means to do so—means which seem limitless to the peasant, who knows that those who have not, are not!

Institutionalized thinking.—To change peasant mentality it is necessary to understand, and to work from within, the peasants' institutional environment. Most peasants do not feel sorry for themselves, or feel beset by insoluble problems unless such factors are pointed out by outside observers who would act as diagnosticians.

1. George M. Foster, "Peasant Society and the Image of Limited Good," in *Peasant Society: A Reader*, eds. Jack M. Potter, May N. Diaz, and George M. Foster (Boston: Little, Brown and Company, 1967), p. 317.

In too many instances, however, "doctors" unfamiliar with the closed social and economic systems of the peasant have, as it were, written prescriptions without understanding—or even talking to— the peasant. The problem of loans, or short-term credit, is an example. A government loan represents a windfall that can be advantageously used, for example, to hire someone else to do work that the *campesino* has usually done himself. He can sit back in the café or *cantina* and watch someone else work, just as the wealthy *patrón* has always done, and this idleness is in no way a threat to community stability. Indeed, he is idle or at least underemployed much of the year. Yet if he uses his loan to buy hybrid seed corn and by planting it increases his yield several fold, he thereby achieves individual progress and by so doing he changes his status, thereby upsetting the status quo and stability of the community, whose fellow members may not sanction such behavior. Such conservative attitudes have spelled survival for the closed peasant community and will continue to be held as long as those communities continue to exist as peasant societies. Once the peasant's view of his social and economic universe is one of expanding opportunity in an open system where initiative is rewarded and not met by negative sanction, he acquires initiative—fast.

Natural and supernatural forces.—The peasant everywhere lives in a world pervaded by fears. His life is hemmed about by taboos, for evil spirits are at work all around him. He may not be able to enter, much less to clear and grow crops on, certain pieces of forest because of the spirit or spirits that live there. He may have to work on an infertile hillside instead of a piece of fertile alluvial river bottom land, over which hovers the ghost of his old friend and compadre, Juan López—for Juan, late one night and full of *aguardiente*, fell face down in the little pond there and breathed his last. In Haiti, the peasant may have to spend much time keeping the voodoo of his enemies off his own plantings and at the same time harnessing those occult forces of black magic for his own ends of bringing discomfiture and bad luck to those who wish him ill. He may have to bury the head of a white rooster in his neighbor's dooryard, or hang the right wing of a guinea hen in the palm tree closest to his door. Thus, phantoms, demons, and horrible apparitions will be called forth to haunt his neighbor.

Fundamental beliefs.—It is important to take into consideration those fundamental beliefs about life and its meaning which are held by the general population. If everyone is basically convinced that what will be will be, then striving for change is futile. The inertia often imputed to tropical peoples, even in the highlands, may be due more to malnutrition, diseases, and parasites than to basic philosophy. They may seem to feel that all things come to him who waits simply because they do not have the energy to stand the process of helping themselves. Further, the conservatism, the resistance to change, that peasants everywhere are said to be imbued with has served as a means of survival, for those near the margin of subsistence dare not take chances with new crops, new techniques, or with anything new. They have to know that any new method must increase their returns, for any decrease might be fatal. They have had to struggle within the way of life that they have evolved, and they should be studied from within that way of life.

Every culture passes on knowledge to the next generation, but the nature of that knowledge suits the survival requirements of the inhabitants of each particular place or region at a particular time.

Geography and history are different threads of the same closely woven fabric that is human society on this earth, and it is very difficult to separate them.

The crux of the whole problem of settlement is to convince pioneers that by accepting innovations and the winds of change, thus moving into new areas and with new technology, they will alter the pattern of their daily lives so to be able to live a more abundant life, spiritually as well as materially.

RURAL-URBAN CLEAVAGE

It is a sad fact that, in the nations of Andean America, the gulf between peasants and urban dwellers has been profound, especially where there is a language barrier as in Ecuador, Peru, and Bolivia. The peasant has not been merely neglected; he has been gratuitously ridiculed and humiliated when not actually physically mishandled, in the army, in church, in the courts, in the post office, and especially in the shops and in the market place.

The average peasant is only mildly surplus- or market-minded, for all too often the trail, road, or river that ties him to the outside world tends to be a one-way street: the products that move over it tend to lose most of their value en route, as the peasant must pay high transportation costs, or high taxes, or suffer outright confiscation at the hands of one who claims to own the land on which the produce was grown. Further, native peoples, ignorant of the official language, who occasionally try to enter the market economy are frequently, and sometimes even openly and flagrantly, robbed by all, even by the small village shopkeepers.

One may witness a scene such as this one. An Indian from a community high in the mountains arrived in a small village of the Andean foothills on market day, his donkey laden with onions, all neatly arranged and tied in bunches convenient for the shopper. Even before the farmer and his donkey arrived at the square where the vendors' stalls were located, the pair was surrounded by a small crowd of people who began pulling bunches of onions off the pack animal, asking the driver in Spanish the price of this bunch or that. The poor man answered hesitantly in broken Spanish only to realize that his interlocutors were moving off with the bunches they had selected; he tried to stem the tide by following one or two persons and stating the price, only to have the thieves pay no attention to him and merely quicken their pace. Meanwhile, others, taking advantage of his having left his patient donkey for a few minutes to plead in vain for payment, just helped themselves. The poor frustrated man came running back to try to stop the open robbery, but the predators tugged and pulled, laughing and shouting at the good fun they were having, and within minutes the whole load of produce was gone. The bewildered peasant, choking with wrath and muttering to himself in Quechua, alone in a hostile, unjust world against which he had no recourse, gradually made his way to the fountain of cool water in the center of the plaza where he bathed his tired feet. For the produce which had cost him so much in time and effort he had nothing to show but feelings of inferiority, rancor, and injustice. He could not take advantage of his day in town to purchase a few necessities and perhaps a drink or two in the local café or bar. There was nothing left for him to do but sit around dejectedly for a few hours, then get astride his animal, and, his heart black with bile and frustration, follow the narrow rocky trail back to his home and family. The only creatures below him in the pecking order are his wife and children, upon whom all too often his suppressed fury is vented. The wife cannot escape, but the children, especially the boys, cannot be expected to tarry at home once they can get out, even run away, to make a living for themselves in the cities, or in the new lands to the east.

Incidents such as this are lessons—part of the educational process —that the poor peasant and his family are quick to learn and slow to forget. When trails, roads, and rivers enjoy two-way traffic, with produce flowing to market in exchange for cash or goods of sufficient value to make the trip worthwhile in the mind of the producer of raw materials, then he will be motivated to further trips to that market—and only then.

MOTIVATION, PRODUCTION, EXCHANGE

In order to escape his own personal closed economic system, his cocoon of self-sufficiency, the peasant or villager must produce something that is saleable, whether it be a bunch of cooking bananas, a load of firewood or charcoal, or a piece of woven goods. If a road is built by the central government, it might be easier for the product to get to market, but both the saleable product and the market are the basic ingredients of a diversified economy—the fundamentals, to be sure. Only when a peasant knows that someone wants and will pay for his products will it, or can it, occur to him that it might be possible to increase his production. He produces a surplus in the first place because he hopes that with it he can get something he wants but cannot produce. The better the peasant is rewarded for whatever surplus he can produce, the more willing is he to accept innovative practices, if by so doing he can increase production.

Unfortunately, millions of human beings, poorly qualified or equipped to cope with modern agricultural problems, are relegated by history and cultural controls to precisely those areas where the problems of soil management are most difficult. Most often those with wealth and training have control over large land tracts of physically good land within easy reach of markets. Such people can apply the techniques of modern scientific management to produce crops for the market, domestic or foreign, and thus achieve a high profit per acre. Further, they are powerful enough to acquire control of other good land to hold for speculative purposes, that is, to hold it at prices which the land would have if it were already settled and being farmed.

In other words, by keeping vast acreages out of production, they are able to price this land out of the market for any small-scale farmer. When access roads are constructed into sparsely settled areas, politicians and speculators often control the very land that the road was ostensibly built to make accessible, with the result that

what was meant to be an access road may even drain out of the
territory the few subsistence farmers already living there!

MOBILITY, ATTITUDES, FACETS OF CHANGE

If new ideas are carefully but unobtrusively planted in what we
smugly think of as a "backward" society, "conservative" attitudes
may possibly change to the extent that the campesino wants to
change; the reaction thus elicited, the new motivation, may make
him reveal capabilities of which he himself had been unaware. The
progressive attitude with which the people who make up the indigenous cultural environment may be imbued might indeed prove
to be more important in development than a grandiose, prefabri-
cated infrastructure inserted in the peasant society by forces foreign
to it.

The education behind this change in attitude is not necessarily
one of formal book learning. Whenever a peasant goes into a
nearby *caserío*, or village, no matter how seldom, he gets new ideas.
Further, it is likely that members of a gang of laborers engaged in
building a road into remote areas are themselves part of the educational process for the few inhabitants living in these sectors. This
was certainly the case with the gangs of laborers who built the railroads in Mexico under Porfirio Diaz. If the campesino is exploited
by those of the village, or by members of the road-building crew,
or by a local landlord or bigwig, he will merely want to get farther
away from them—either by moving into a distant urban center or
by going ever more deeply into the protecting forest.

Vast changes in habits and attitudes are already under way. Today, one may meet a barefoot campesino on a national airline with
his prize fighting cock under his arm or in a makeshift cage, on his
way to the weekend cockfights in a neighboring town. He will be
paring the spurs or plucking the leg and neck feathers of his pet,
with as much nonchalance as if he were at home. Such an en-
counter would have been unthinkable a few decades ago.

Channels of communication opened up in the past few decades
now link the campesino to the larger national society and even to
some extent to the world outside. The recent network of roads has
vastly extended the horizon of the peasant, beckoning him to leave
his smoke-filled, malodorous, flea- or bug-ridden hovel, where he
and his family live in friendly symbiosis with his domestic animals.
If the siren call has not been strong enough for the pater familias,

it often has been effective in luring away the sons and daughters. By the tens of thousands they have gone to the city where they have run into that almost impenetrable wall of joblessness characteristic of pre-industrial, urban agglomerations. But some have followed the trails and roads to the virgin tropical lands of the east.

This migration, largely into the Oriente, this slowly growing exodus to new lands and new hopes, is our concern in this book.[2]

HISTORICAL BACKGROUND

Never in the history of the world were there events comparable to the discovery and exploration of the New World by the Spaniards and Portuguese. The first sight of the shores, covered with heavy tropical forest or sand dunes and giant cactus, must have been a wondrous thing to these adventurous men of action. They were not philosophical over what they saw, for their compulsion was to dominate what they came in contact with, whether man or nature, animate or inanimate. Hungry for gold and glory, in the course of two generations they had crossed deserts and penetrated rain forests. The Spaniards dismembered the Inca and Aztec empires, began to indoctrinate the conquered people with Christianity, and sent galleons of fabulous treasure back to Spain. And they gradually became aware of the outlines of the main physical features of what is now South America, with its huge chain of mountains—the Andes —and its vast, tropical, forested heartland—the trackless, almost uninhabited Amazon and Orinoco lowlands east of the Andes.

At the time of the Conquest, the plains Indians of what is now Venezuela lived in villages, or caseríos, widely distributed over the *llanos*. In the selection of sites for these settlements, the available supply of food and water had been the dominant factor, especially for the Caribs. However, as the Achaguas and other Arawak tribes were pushed from the rivers by the fierce Caribs, they probably sought out easily defended or easily vacated sites. The pre-Columbian causeways and watch towers in the vicinity of Ciudad Bolivia–

2. Isaiah Bowman, in his classic volume *The Pioneer Fringe*, made no mention of the lowland humid tropics; he did not consider them a potential pioneering zone. The area east of the Andes is an excellent example of the penetration and settlement of the humid tropical lowlands during the forty years since the publication of *The Pioneer Fringe*, the last great land frontier zone on earth. As will be seen, failures of settlement and colonization schemes have resulted less from the influence of physical and cultural factors than from socioeconomic reality which lost out to sociopolitical expediency.

Barinas State, as well as the ridged fields mentioned by Castellanos, were undoubtedly built by the quiet, hard-working, agricultural Arawaks, possibly for purposes of defense.[3] The Caribs, bent on conquest, came up the rivers in dug-out canoes. From the river it would be almost impossible to see the enemies' settlements in the open savanna because of the gallery forest. Even when seen, it would be difficult to effect a surprise attack. Besides, the causeways could be used by the Arawaks for flight or for bringing in reserves. In the dry season, the Caribs, adept on the water, would be forced to cross a large open savanna on foot before battle. Thus, the attackers would be placed at a disadvantage in many ways. At all events, the Arawaks did not hesitate to settle in the savannas despite the tremendous work involved in building these great earthen structures.

On the north (left) bank of the Orinoco, immediately below the influx of the Apure, there were Indian settlements which were famed among the Orinoco Indians because of the fertility of their soil and the abundance of their food supplies. When the Orinoco subsides at the beginning of the dry season, a deposit of fine, fertile silt is left behind, in the same manner as the deposit left by the Nile after its annual overflow. Padre Gumilla relates how various tribes—Otomacos, Guamos, Paos, and Serrucos—were cultivating in this fertile deposit a kind of maize which matured in two months. But great agricultural activity had been carried on by the aboriginal Indians; as early as 1534, when Herrera's expedition arrived at Cabruta, his soldiers found "in caves which they had made in low knolls a large quantity of maize which they must have kept there to avoid the inundations of the river."[4] Maize yielded well, for these farming people had become such epicures that corn on the cob was a favorite dish. "In truth, so much is eaten when the ears still have tender grains, that the Indians themselves notably decrease their harvests [of ripe ears]."[5]

There was a very important trade route for gold which followed the Front Ranges along the southeastern slopes of the Venezuelan Andes. The excellent water supply and the fertile alluvial soil along this route made possible a rather dense Indian population. There were numerous thriving hamlets. Along this route, gold from the Chibcha domain, probably even from the Inca Empire, went

3. Juan de Castellanos, *Elegías de varones ilustres de Indias*, 1:539.
4. Sven Lovén, "The Orinoco in Old Indian Times," 2:716.
5. Joseph Gumilla, *El Orinoco ilustrado*, p. 279.

to Venezuela, eventually sent as far east as Barcelona, Maracapana, and Cumaná. Lovén suggests that there were large amounts of gold in the uplands of Cumaná because the Indians there raised coca, for which their neighbors eagerly traded gold.[6] On this route, Tenauren (now Turén), just east of the Portuguesa River, seems to have been the point farthest east where gold was cast. The Achaguas, a branch of the Arawaks, inhabited the strip of land just east of the Cordillera, the greater part of which was above the annual inundations suffered by the lower llanos. They were peace-loving and industrious and had come in friendly contact with the cultured Chibchas. As a result of contact with this affluent people, they had become the chief traders in gold between the people of the plateau and those of the llanos and northeastern Venezuela.

Eastern Ecuador has for long been a kind of *terra incognita*, especially from the view of archaeology. Parts of this area have recently been most successfully and profitably studied by Father Pedro Porras Garcés, who has built up in the town of his birth, Ambato, an archaeological museum with emphasis on the culture of the Quitus and the Pansaleos. During his many apostolic missions he has found traces of man's occupance in what is now dense forest. He has carried out explorations covering thousands of square miles over a period of more than six years in these forests, beginning in the vicinity of Papallacta, gradually extending farther eastward into the Valley of the Quijos River and into the Valley of the Misagualli, a tributary of the Napo.

The pottery of Quijos shows that there were close commercial ties with the people of the Ecuadorian *altiplano*, that there was some trade in Loja with the Paltas or Jíbaros of the Catamayo Valley. Perhaps there was also some interchange with the zone of Tierradentro in Colombia, where the great monuments of San Agustín are found.

It is possible that the Valley of Quijos was the final stronghold of cultures of the central inter-Andean Valley of Ecuador whose inhabitants emigrated eastward as a result of the Incaic invasions. Here in the east they built fortifications which they had not felt necessary in their high heartland. The armies of the Incas were afraid of the hot tropics and, except for short military forays, did not penetrate such lands either in coastal Ecuador or in the east.

6. Lovén, "The Orinoco in Old Indian Times," p. 719.

In the vicinity of Papallacta, simple tombs were found. The dead were buried in excavations in the ground, or wells, and in cavities in rocks or protected by overhanging rocks. Farther afield, particularly beyond Baeza, prehistoric roads, great cyclopean walls, and monoliths covered with strange figures and symbols have been discovered, as well as agricultural terraces, fortresses, tombs of many descriptions, and what seem to be boundary markers or dolmens.[7]

In the Llanos de Mojos of northeastern Bolivia, pre-Conquest aboriginal people achieved the most intensive utilization of tropical grasslands known in the history of the New World. The tribes of Mojos adapted to annual flooding by constructing various types of earthworks to provide dry ground for dwellings, cultivation, and communication. The drained fields, some 50,000 acres, are a monument to savanna agriculture in what is now northeastern Bolivia; they were estimated to have supported several hundred thousand people up to the seventeenth century.[8] From 1682 to 1767, settlements were founded, but the population was rapidly reduced by European diseases, and the native cultures of the Arawak-speaking Mojo and Baure Indians deteriorated.

It is significant that in this harsh savanna environment, where floods alternate with droughts, pre-Spanish peoples with extremely primitive techniques achieved a productivity and population density which have not since been equaled. Since savanna cultivation is less productive and perhaps requires more labor than shifting forest cultivation, Denevan suggests that, since stone for tools was rare, it may have actually been easier to raise earth in savanna land than it was to clear forest.[9] It is further suggested that population may have become so dense that there was not enough forest available to support successful shifting cultivation based on a long forest fallow. As in the Venezuelan llanos, tribal territorial claims may have prevented migration and thereby necessitated intensive cultivation of whatever land was available. At all events, savanna farming was given up early in the colonial period, for the Conquest introduced metal tools for clearing forest, drastically reduced the population, and established new groupings of the Indians.

7. Pedro I. Porras Garcés, *Contribución al estudio de la arqueología e historia de los Valles Quijos y Misagualli (Alto Napo) en la región oriental del Ecuador, S.A.*, p. 32.

8. William M. Denevan, *The Aboriginal Cultural Geography of the Llanos de Mojos of Bolivia*, pp. 90, 96.

9. Ibid., pp. 94–95.

The sixteenth-century explorers of the Amazon, such as Orellana and Orsua and Aguirre, provisioned themselves from the food supplies of the Indians they met, commandeered their canoes, and took into slavery those that they wanted. The result was—very early—a complete breakdown in native life and an appalling decrease in the Indian population. By the mid-eighteenth century, Portuguese slavers were doing a thriving business, capturing Indian slaves in the upper reaches of the Amazon and its tributaries and selling them to plantation owners downriver or along the east coast. Von Humboldt noted that along the banks of the Cassiquiare River, or "Canal," which connects the Orinoco and Negro rivers, the Indians had fled the slavers and taken refuge in the bush to the east.

Even as late as the mid-nineteenth century, the English explorer Bates remarked on the common but illegal practice of obtaining Indian children as slaves from the wild tribes of the interior. And H. H. Rusby, writing of his experiences, observed: "At the time of the occurrences which I have related [1885], these Indians [Arauna Indians of the Ibon] were a large and powerful tribe, occupying a wide area of country. In the meantime the aggressions of the whites, not merely by the invasion of their territory, but through the raids for prisoners to be enslaved as peon workmen in the rubber industry, have resulted in their almost complete annihilation."[10]

As late as 1906, Colonel Fawcett wrote of the wholesale capture of wild Indians who were enslaved to work tapping rubber; it was plentiful and brought a high price on the world market, but was difficult to get at because rubber trees were scattered over a huge area and increasing toil was necessary to locate and work them. Women and children were wantonly butchered, as were any men who became ill or who could not gather their assigned quota. Colonel Fawcett's observations of conditions in eastern Bolivia bear out completely Sir Roger Casement's report on the shocking conditions on the Putumayo River in eastern Colombia a few years later. And according to newspaper reports, such activities have by no means ceased in the remote areas of tropical South America.

The white man, bearer of civilization, did not superimpose a new technological order on tropical South America. Rather, he enslaved the Indians and forcibly made them continue a gathering economy, the profits of which resounded to the benefit of the over-

10. H. H. Rusby, *Jungle Memories* (New York, 1935), pp. 297–98.

lord, not the Indian. Thus, the primitive gathering economy was largely frozen as found. As long as those countries controlling these "primitive" tropical areas were content with a gathering-economy status quo, there could be no change.

During the past half century, the world has experienced a revolution of rising expectations to which the peoples of densely populated Andean America have not been immune. They have begun to break their medieval bonds. Geographic and social mobility are increasing, effecting massive changes in the distribution of population and in the manner of living.

ALTITUDINAL LIFE ZONES

Mountains everywhere modify the climate, since temperatures are lowered by about 3 degrees for every 1,000 feet elevation. What is thought of as the true tropics is found from sea level to an elevation of about 3,000 feet, and this altitudinal life zone is referred to as *tierra caliente,* or hot country. From there to 6,000–8,000 feet (depending on angle of slope and hours of sunshine), there is a modified tropical climate; the sectors between those contours are known as *tierra templada,* or temperate country. Above this contour is *tierra fría,* or cold country, where night temperatures of near freezing, and occasionally even below, are succeeded during the day by shade temperatures in the fifties. The great mass of Andean Indians and mestizos still live in the tierra fría of the altiplano (the high plateau between the eastern and western Andean Cordilleras) and in the high valleys. From their ranks come a majority of the settlers of the pioneer fringe zones in the humid tropics.

TROPICAL GRASSLANDS OR SAVANNAS

The humid tropical sector between Venezuela and Bolivia consists largely of grassy savannas in Venezuela, eastern Colombia, and much of Bolivia. These sectors have a distinct dry season (*verano*) during periods of low sun, and rains fall during the wet season (*invierno*), the period of high sun. Even in these grasslands rivers are lined by gallery forests varying in width from several hundred yards to a mile or more. Land that is very steep or stony induces rapid runoff of precipitation; sandy soils may be extremely permeable; in such areas, even where precipitation is heavy and well distributed, edaphic savannas of coarse grasses may result.

TROPICAL RAIN FORESTS OR SELVAS

True rain forest is found where rainfall is heavy (usually 80 to 100 inches or more) and well distributed throughout the year. This is what is usually called jungle. This is the world of giant buttressed trees festooned with lianas and laden with epiphytes that produce here and there brilliant red or white flowers that gleam in the dark foliage. Even on sunny days the forest canopy shuts out most of the sunlight. When it rains, great drops patter loudly on the millions of leaves and then drip from leaf to leaf to the ground floor; this is a dim twilight world of greens and browns and dampness, of rotting, termite-infested wood and of wet, soggy vegetation. The layer of leaf mould on the ground is thin or nonexistent because of the rapid rate of oxidation. Soluble salts have been leached out and the resultant acid soil is well adapted to the growth of trees and shrubs. Such forest-covered land is extremely difficult to clear, especially for a person armed with only a machete or an axe. The clearing of such forests on steep slopes makes the soil a prey to rapid erosion.

FROM TROPICAL RAIN FOREST TO PASTURELAND

When such forests on hill lands are cleared for the growing of crops, erosion would be even worse than it is if it were not for the fact that aggressively colonizing species of perennial African grasses, readily disseminated by seed or cutting, have been widely and rapidly naturalized in the forestlands of humid tropical America. Areas newly cleared of forest, cropped for a few years, are either planted to grass or invaded by an aggressive volunteer grass. Crop agriculture is thus just a step in the process of converting forestland into pastureland.

Such grasses also compete successfully with native grasses that evolve under very low grazing pressure. A case in point, Yaragúa, or Jaragúa (*Hyparrhenia rufa*), has been able to compete with native savanna grasses in the Venezuelan llanos due to its aggressiveness and ability to self-seed. This African invader, apparently aided by being regularly burned, within a decade or two may well be the dominant grass in the open Venezuelan llanos, where it is fired each year in the dry season and grazed closely during the rainy season to prevent its becoming rank and fibrous.

Melinis minutiflora, or molasses grass, so named for its characteristic molasses-like odor and the gummy exudations that make its hairy leaves sticky, has spread rapidly since its introduction into the Santa Marta area of Colombia, quickly escaping from cultivation to become a volunteer in abandoned coffee fields and road cuts, as well as in pastures dominated by native grasses. It is continuing to expand rapidly as a result of continuing forest destruction, clearing of second growth, and dry-season fires set by man. In Blydenstein's recent study of the Colombian llanos, he identifies a "Melinis minutiflora association" on the highest terraces and foothills at the base of the Andes.[11]

Pará grass (*Brachiaria mutica* [*Panicum purpurascens*]) spreads chiefly by runners and is partial to the poorly drained bottom lands of the hot humid tropics (tierra caliente). It reached the Cauca Valley in the 1860s and today is found everywhere in the American tropics on moist, poorly drained soils. It is to be found along the new penetration roads that reach down from the Andes into the Amazonian lowlands and in abandoned fields in low-lying areas along those roads.

Good grazing grasses serve to develop under grazing pressure, and African grasses have probably had such pressure since the Pleistocene; they simply stand up better to grazing and have higher nutritive value than native species. Regrettable as it may be from the point of view of the conservationist, it is a fact that tropical rain forests are disappearing over vast areas and are being replaced by African grasses. Perhaps one should rejoice at the invasion of the vigorous aggressive African grasses in the humid tropics; they are an important factor in the control of erosion and they are "at the base of the new hope for the development of a viable commercial livestock industry in the low latitudes of the New World tropics."[12]

11. James J. Parsons, "Spread of African Pasture Grasses to the American Tropics," *Journal of Range Management* 25 (January 1972) :15.
12. Ibid., p. 17.

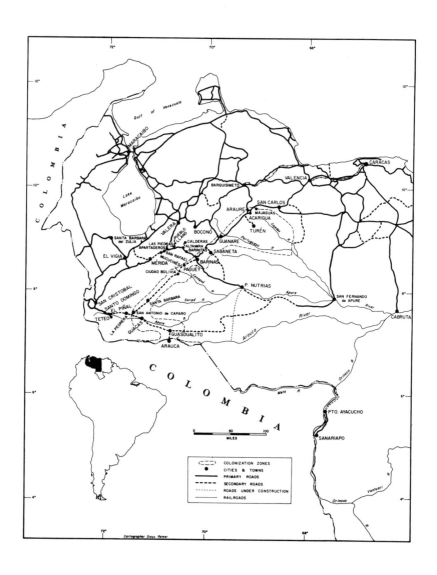

Cartographer Sious Remer

2. Venezuela

V ENEZUELA was the first part of South America to be discovered and explored by Europeans. The early explorations of its
vast interior were carried out by Germans working for the banking
firm of Welser, under a concession of the King of Spain. Largely
neglected by Spain as a colony, a prey to ruthless tyrants during
the first century of political independence, Venezuela achieved international importance in the twentieth century for its wealth in
oil and iron ore.

THE LLANOS-ANDES BORDER

In tropical Latin America generally, population has been concentrated in the cool to cold highlands and has until recently tended
to avoid the once disease-ridden humid lowlands. Venezuela is no
exception to this general pattern. The three distinct altitudinal life
zones, *tierra caliente* (hot country), *tierra templada* (temperate
country), and *tierra fría* (cold country), all are easily distinguish-
able. In the cold, desolate *páramo* country above the tree line, sheep
graze and low, stunted shrubs are gathered for fuel.

In the Venezuelan Andes, the cold country between 6,000 and
12,000 feet above sea level, population pressure has long forced an
overintensive exploitation of agricultural resources. Thousands of
people expend all their energies to make enough food for bare
survival.

The upper limits of cultivation were reached long ago, and there
has been a stream of migrants going to small regional centers and to
cities such as Maracaibo, Carácas, and Valencia. But thousands
have migrated to the rugged Andean foothills and to the great
plains, or *llanos*, particularly in the last several decades.

The llanos, the great plains of Venezuela, are tropical grasslands,
or savannas, green and lush in the wet season, parched in the dry

17

season. These extensive grassy plains have been the traditional cattle country of Venezuela. The llanos-Andes border zone is in a period of economic transition. Because of oil revenues, modern technological methods are being introduced in agriculture and animal husbandry. The history of this area provides a background for understanding the contemporary scene.

Historical background.—The pre-Columbian inhabitants of the llanos-Andes border area practiced a primitive patch agriculture, supplemented by hunting and fishing. Deer, tapirs, wild hogs, and capybaras abounded on the grassy plains and in the gallery forests along the rivers, which yielded fish and turtles in great quantities. According to the noted scholar Sven Lovén, gold from the Chibcha domain in the Bogotá area was carried along the well-established trade route through the Andes-llanos border area to be exchanged for the coca leaves produced by the Indians of Cumaná.[1] Along the coast north and east of Barquisimeto, salt was gathered from nat-ural—and perhaps from artificial—evaporating pans and was traded along this same route to the Indians of the interior. Nikolaus Fed-ermann wrote in 1530 that Hacarigua was a group of many hamlets situated near one another at the edge of the plains, where "we were well received; they gave us gold, game, and all kinds of provisions."[2]

Although the area was somewhat neglected during the colonial era, as early as 1610 the landholders of the mountains found it ad-vantageous to bring the Indian workers whom they held *encomienda* down to the plains where the soils were more fertile. Here tobacco, cotton, cacao, indigo, and corn were grown. In 1606 a *Real Cédula* prohibited the growing of tobacco in all of Venezuela except the remote province of Barinas, 240 miles from the coast, on a broad piedmont alluvial fan at the southern foot of the Andes. This measure was intended to stop contraband trade in tobacco and gave an impetus to its cultivation that continued long after the cédula was abrogated, six years later.

Barinas flourished under the colonial regime, from about 1750 to the Wars of Independence in the early nineteenth century. It was a market for the cattle and horses raised on the great plains. Rice, sugar, corn, bananas, yuca, and vegetables were grown for local use and tobacco, indigo, and cacao for export. According to the census of 1787, there were half a million cattle and a hundred thousand

1. Lovén, "The Orinoco in Old Indian Times," p. 719.
2. Marco-Aurelio Vila, *Aspectos geográficos del Estado Portuguesa*, p. 7.

horses and mules in the territory that is now the state of Barinas. This was the period of maximum development, when it was generally said that in all the expanse of the llanos there were no poor people.

Then came the Wars of Independence, followed during the latter half of the nineteenth century by a series of disastrous revolutions and internecine civil wars; both the human and animal populations diminished greatly in numbers. This unsettled state of affairs led many families to migrate from the llanos-Andes border zone into the Cordillera de los Andes, which increased considerably in population. The state of Zamora, now Barinas, has recovered only in the past few years. It had 62,696 inhabitants in 1891, only 55,055 in the 1920 census, but 80,503 in 1950 and 139,271 in 1961.[3] The estimated population in 1972 was around 200,000.

In 1907 the llanos-Andes border area was visited by Hiram Bingham (later a United States Senator), who desired to explore the route by which Bolívar in 1819 had conducted his liberating army across Venezuela and Colombia. Bingham's observations appeared in book form under the title *The Journal of an Expedition across Venezuela and Colombia, 1906–1907.* Some excerpts from this volume, written by a keen observer, show the backward condition of the country in those days.

> Two leagues south of the Portuguesa is Guanare, once the capital of the State of Zamora, but now reduced to a quiet somnolence that gives no promise of being disturbed for many years to come. The latest official figures give it a population of thirty thousand. But as there are only five very small shops and certainly not three hundred houses standing, it is difficult to account for more than two thousand residents. I doubt very much if there are fifteen hundred (p. 59).
>
> A mile beyond the river we came to the picturesque ruins of the old Tocupido church. One of the arches is still standing, but a tree twenty or thirty years old is growing in the aisle. Thirty thatched huts and a small church with a little thatched belfry, a deserted plaza and a few coconut trees are all that is left of this old Spanish town... (p. 62).
>
> Barinas was founded earlier than Carácas, the Spaniards having explored this part of Venezuela before they penetrated the region immediately south of the Coast Range. The city

3. Venezuela, Ministerio de Fomento, *Noveno censo general de población* (Caracas, 1968), p. 131.

prospered greatly during the Colonial epoch and was famous for its tobacco, which commanded a high price in the German markets. Barinas was at that time the capital of the province. One of the Government buildings is still standing, and presents a fine appearance. There are probably not more than one thousand people living here now. I presume six hundred would be a closer estimate. The official figures give it twenty-five hundred. It once had ten thousand inhabitants.

In the latter part of the eighteenth century a great cattle king, who had social ambitions, built himself a palace here. During the wars with Spain he assisted the Loyalists and was made a marquis for his pains. The ruins of his great establishment, the "Marquisate," are most interesting. The house measures 138 by 114 feet. The roof is gone and much of the rich ornamentation, but the grand court is surrounded by columns which are still standing. There were seventeen rooms besides the hallways. Other large ruins in the vicinity, and many mounds scattered through the city, might be explored with profit.

Barinas is the last city we shall see for some time. It is like the other cities of the Western Llanos, San Carlos, Araure, and Guanare. All bear witness of a departed greatness. In the last days of the Colonial epoch there must have been at least ten times as many people here. Those that remain are poor and unenterprising. Apathy is their most marked characteristic. Their houses are generally built of adobe, sometimes with red-tiled roofs but more often with palm-leaf thatch. Their churches are in a better state of preservation than might have been expected. Yet one sees very few signs of superstition. Schools of a primary grade are common in the towns and every one seems to be able to read and write . . . (pp. 67–69).

Recent regional developments.—The rapid substitution in recent decades of a market economy for the traditional subsistence economy of rural Venezuela has been nowhere more marked than in the area southeast of the Andes, particularly in the transition zone between plains and Andes of which Barinas and Guanare are regional and administrative capitals.

Two decades after Bingham's historic trek, the senior author worked in the llanos-Andes border area and published some of his findings in a paper entitled "Along the Llanos-Andes Border in Zamora, Venezuela." The introductory paragraph reads:

Some of the communities of South America now have a relatively lower position than they enjoyed in the colonial days. Such is the state of Zamora in Venezuela, whose capital, Barinas, was once second only to Carácas in size and importance. The prime cause of its backwardness is assuredly the poor state of communications, discouraging alike immigration of foreigners and enterprise on the part of the native inhabitants. Here is a state with an area of 13,500 square miles —larger than Massachusetts and Connecticut—and a population density of only four to the square mile (1926), almost the lowest rank among the Venezuelan states. The roads within the state itself and those connecting it with external centers are practically intransitable in the wet season. The automobile road from Pedraza (Ciudad Bolivia) to Acarigua is open only five months of the year, and even then one may be delayed in fording a flooded stream. From May to November, inclusive, travel in any degree of personal comfort is impossible. Necessary traffic in freight is carried by pack trains which cross the mountains in the Santo Domingo Valley to connect with the great Transandine Highway. A little freight comes in *bongos*, dugout canoes, up the rivers Canaguá, Suripá, and Santo Domingo from the Apure. Mule carts come from Acarigua to Barinas in a week or ten days over water-soaked roads. This shows how necessary is the completion of the road under construction from Acarigua, Portuguesa, to San Cristóbal, Táchira. Except in a few places, the road, the Carretera Occidental, follows a major physiographic boundary—that between the Llanos and the mountains (p. 411).

Passages from the writer's diary, published in a later then-and-now study, give first impressions of the changes wrought during the past few decades:

Barinas, August 4. From Acarigua to Barinas there were many rice fields along the road, dry, or unirrigated, rice on grasslands that but a few years ago were practically valueless. Near Boconó rice fields were being harvested, by combine harvesters. The growers were taking advantage of the dry season to effect the harvest. Floating laborers were coming to Guanare from Acarigua, looking for work. In so many places, even in the country, the traditional thatch roof is being replaced by aluminum sheeting, which costs more in the beginning but which lasts much longer than thatch.

Barinas, August 5. I can hardly believe my eyes. This place
has changed, considering what it was when I was here before,
even more than Carácas. The nicely paved streets, lined by
big clean stores with huge refrigerators and equipped with
neon signs, are lighted by electric lights. The town boasts
running water which is purified and stored in a huge tank
north of town. The ruins of the old "Marquisate" of the Marquis de Boconó, a malodorous pest hole overgrown with weeds
and brush till 1936, have now been transformed into an attractive modern building which houses the state government
offices. The two squares between this building and the cathe-
dral, formerly paved with white cobblestones between which
grass grew abundantly, is now a lovely, well-tended park. The
town has expanded five or six blocks in every direction, except
to the east where it is bounded inconveniently close by the
Santo Domingo River. The Hotel Internacional is a clean,
efficiently run place where excellent meals are served. It is
north of town in what was formerly a pasture. It is a wonderful little place in which to stay, after what one could expect
so far back-country—owned and managed by an Italian, it has
excellent beds, is neat and clean, and is being enlarged to take
care of fifteen or twenty more guests. The Italian influence
in particular and the European influence in general is most
welcome as a leaven in some of these back country, down-at-
the-heel towns or villages. For instance, many of the stores,
furniture factories, tailor shops, are run by Europeans, who
bring in new ideas of cleanliness, attractive presentation of
wares, cheerful service, and so on. The town is growing
rapidly from local immigration; people come from the small
Llano settlements, from the mountains, even from coastal
Venezuela and from certain parts of Colombia. No wonder.
There's money to be made here. Just outside of town are two
sawmills with modern equipment, as well as huge storage and
milling facilities for rice. Much cement block construction is
going on. Here are schools and hospitals, education and medical facilities that are unobtainable elsewhere. It is hard to believe that this thriving, bustling center is the same lifeless,
forgotten village I saw in 1931.[4]

Observations made by the senior author four decades ago are
revealing:

4. Crist, "Along the Llanos-Andes Border in Venezuela: Then and Now," p.
194.

In the Suripá woodlands cacao grows wild. Cultivated it would yield enormously. In colonial days the cacao and tobacco from Barinas and Pedraza were considered the best in Venezuela, but the latter is little grown now, and only enough of the former is gathered for local use. The word *Varinas*, incorporated in the German language and signifying a good brand of tobacco, testifies to the former wide renown of the Barinas product. Delicious oranges are grown in Pedraza; yet there are comparatively few trees there, and no attempt at all is made to form large orchards. Near the most important towns, Barinas, Pedraza (Ciudad Bolivia), Santa Bárbara, Sabaneta, and Puerto Nutrias, corn, rice, yuca, and bananas are the main crops.

The towns of Altamira, Las Calderas, and Barinitas are the most important ones in the mountainous area. The crops that to a great extent sustain their populations are beans, potatoes, yuca, and cane. Coffee is the export crop.

There are excellent sites at narrow parts of the great rivers— this is particularly true of the Santo Domingo near Altamira[5] —where dams could be constructed to furnish power.

Tanneries for curing cow and alligator hides could do a great business in supplying the home markets with good leather, which now must be imported (pp. 421–22).

The Santo Domingo River occupies an old line of weakness along which there has been much faulting, and doubtless for this reason the river has cut farther headward than the others draining southeast from the Mérida Range.

The relatively low passes across the cordillera at the head of the Santo Domingo and a tributary, the Apartaderos and Timotes passes, respectively, have from remote times been favorable to trade between the llanos and the Mérida region. On the fertile terraces along this rather easy route fair-sized towns have grown up and serve as way stations for the numerous pack trains (pp. 419–20).[6]

Transportation.—In the field of transportation great strides have been made in valorizing the rich resources of grassland and forest, of plain and mountain. The Acarigua-Barinas section of the highway is excellent, a good all-weather road, asphalted all the way. All

5. This dam is now a reality.
6. They also served as way stations for migrants in their gradual descent from the bleak cold lands of the high mountains to the more hospitable country in the foothills and plains to the south.

the rivers have been bridged. The Barinas-Apartaderos section has recently been completed. A trip that formerly took three days on muleback is now made comfortably in five or six hours by car, or one hour by plane. The construction of this highway has put the area south of Lake Maracaibo in economic contact with Valencia and Carácas. Scores of truckloads of plantains from the rich lands between El Vigía and Santa Bárbara del Zulia move over this road instead of the one through Valera and Barquisimeto.

The road from Barinas via Ciudad Bolivia to Santa Bárbara de Barinas has now opened up a vast area for lumbering and for settlement, namely the huge tract known as the Suripá woodlands, a great triangle with Santa Bárbara, Santa Rosalía, and Ciudad Bolivia as the apices. Trucks, jeeps, and buses can reach Santa Bárbara from the Transandean Highway at San Cristóbal, via Puerto Teteo and San Antonio de Caparo. For both economic and strategic reasons it was important for Venezuela to pave (1966) the Barinas–San Cristóbal highway along the llanos-Andes border and thus open up to settlement this rich but sparsely populated region.

One of the unexpected developments in transportation on the llanos is the growing number of bicycles. Formerly the *llanero*, the plainsman, old or young, had to have a horse. Now he gets about on a bicycle, except in the very rainy weather. But the paths and wheel tracks dry up so rapidly that a bicycle can be used almost the year round. Bicycle riding is in large part a response, on the part of a people with more and more money to spend, to the fast-growing mileage of good asphalt roads.

Lumbering.—In the senior author's 1932 paper he wrote of

> ... many kinds of timber available both for coarse constructional needs and for houses and furniture. Mahogany is found, as well as the large *cedro* (*Cedrela mexicana* Roem.) which has an easily worked, durable wood from which the dugouts are commonly made. The *almácigo* (*Bursera simaruba*) is also found in large quantities. This tree, when tapped, gives forth a sweet-smelling resin which is used as an ointment and is burned for incense.
>
> From the *palma llanera* or *palma de sombrero* (*Copenicia Tectorum* Mart.) come the leaves that are universally used for the roofs of houses and the young leaves from which broad-brimmed hats are made. The heavy trunks are used for various building purposes, and the fruit for chicken and hog feed.

The leaves of the *yagua* (*Attalea* var. sp.) are also used for roofing, and its nuts yield a fine oil. The trunk, when tapped, gives forth a sap that soon turns into a fine-tasting potent wine. Nuts from the coco palm (*Cocos nucifera*) and *corozo* (*Acrocomia sclerocarpa*) are gathered for their rich oil content. The stately *saman* (*Samanea saman* Mer.) is planted for its shade. The *totuma* (*Crescentia cujete* L.) trees yield the fruits of the same name from whose hard shells all sorts of household articles are made.

The lumber industry is now booming. In the forests west of Ciudad Bolivia (Barinas Province) are still to be found large examples of *cedro* (*Cedrela mexicana* Roemer) and *caoba* (*Swietenia Candollei* Pittier). *Roble* (*Platymiscium* sp.), another hardwood, is also exploited for its fine wood. A valuable softwood is *ceiba* (*Ceiba pentandra* Gaertn.) which is used in making boxes and matches.

Population movements.—After the Wars of Independence the former slaves and the poor and landless had neither the techniques nor the experience to take over and operate the ruined haciendas. They fled to the villages and towns, where they eked out precarious livelihoods and where they were fairly safe from the marauding revolutionary bands that continued to devastate the country for nearly a century. But now that roads are being built, the wealthy cattle rancher or rice farmer does not have to live in the city; with little time and trouble he can drive to town and return in his car, jeep, or truck. His existence has ceased to be one long frustrated sigh for city life, because he can now afford to have installed on his ranch some of the conveniences of urban living, such as electric or gasoline lights, running water, and sanitary facilities. The stream of rural migrants to the urban areas, evident for a century and at its peak during the past two decades, may begin to recede when life in the country becomes materially more rewarding and physically more satisfying.

Movements of population between the mountains and foothills and the plains are not new in the llanos-Andes border area. In the latter half of the nineteenth century—indeed, up to a generation ago—there was a mountainward movement, due mainly to political unrest. Another reason was the prevalence of disease, particularly malaria and a virulent form of fever known as *la económica* because it reportedly killed its victims so fast they did not have time to call a doctor. People who could do so left the lower hot country for the relatively disease-free mountains. However, a sustained health campaign, the influence of which is felt in the remotest parts of the country, has been a boon to the area. Forty years ago Barinas and its vicinity were spoken of as a most unhealthful place, but today malaria is practically unknown. The war against mosquitoes has destroyed the vectors of infection, and the widespread use of anti-malarial specifics is another contributing factor. Further, few people nowadays suffer from tropical ulcers or yaws or from the unsightly skin disease known as "carare" or "carate." The incidence of diseases such as amoebic dysentery and typhoid fever has greatly lessened as pure drinking water has been provided for villages. Most ranchers now have drilled wells that supply uncontaminated water. Formerly water for household use was dipped out of the nearest pond or stream. Tropical anemia due to hookworm infestation is on the decline since the wearing of shoes has become more widespread. Infant mortality has decreased.

As public health measures were introduced, and particularly as the campaign against the mosquito became felt in the rapid decrease in malaria, mountaineers again began to descend from their steep, rocky, and infertile fields to the richer lands in the foothills and on the plains. The movement is often carried out in two stages. Residents at elevations of 8,000 feet or more move into unoccupied farmland at 4,000 to 6,000 feet, and those living at the lower elevations move into the Front Ranges or even into the llanos. Hamlets or small towns at intermediate elevations, such as Boconó, Calderas, Altamira, and Barinitas, with their tributary areas, lose population to the llanos at the same time that they receive migrants from the higher Andes.

The construction of highways and the institution of bus service have promoted geographical mobility. The Mérida-Barinas highway serves as a corridor for migrants from Las Piedras or Pueblo Llano, or even from San Rafael and Mucuchíes on the other side of the mountains, who settle near Altamira or Barinitas. Here they raise corn, yuca, dasheens, and lentils for home use and coffee for market; they also keep a few chickens and fatten a hog or two. They are able to compete successfully with farmers already living in that zone, who frequently find it advantageous to move to the lower foothills or into the llanos.

On the Barinas–Ciudad Bolivia section of the piedmont, small settlements have come into being in areas formerly uninhabited. Curbatí, Corozo, and Paguéy, at one time only a house or two, are now hamlets of forty or fifty families. And the people are prosperous, in contrast with the poverty of two generations ago in the mountains and in the foothills. It is fairly easy to hack out clearings in the gallery forests along the rivers and in a few months get a crop of corn to fatten hogs, which can be sold on the hoof and shipped to market by truck. Forested, or partly forested, areas, with their fertile alluvial soils and a high water table, with transportation facilities are the first to be cleared and settled.

The valleys of the Santo Domingo and Boconó rivers are areas of dispersed settlement par excellence. Here the life zones depend on altitude, number of hours of sunshine, angle of slope, soil properties, and so on, producing a highly complex agricultural landscape. The physiognomy of the cultural landscape is further complicated by the fact that the inhabitants live dispersed in the countryside and work fragmented holdings on different kinds of soils, in many cases in different climatic zones. For example, corn and beans will be grown around a house, potatoes on a plot a thousand feet or more higher, and cooking bananas several thousand feet lower. Seemingly minor physical factors, such as local winds, affect the altitudinal dispersal of fields and crops. These dispersed settlements whose inhabitants work fragmented holdings would offer a fruitful field of investigation.

La Yuca, between Barinas and Ciudad Bolivia, is a settlement (*caserío*[7]) of fifteen or twenty houses, a quarter of a mile or so apart. The inhabitants visit back and forth and perform agricultural and household tasks together. The function of this loose grouping of the houses seems to be to facilitate visiting; other urban functions are lacking.

Foreign immigrants to Venezuela are playing a role out of proportion to their total numbers. Tens of thousands of Italians and thousands of Spanish and Portuguese immigrants have entered the country since World War II. Voluntary European immigration has increased as wages have risen, but the newcomers have steadfastly refused to be merely a reservoir of cheap labor to be employed by the landowners during peak seasons only and left jobless, homeless,

7. The *caserío* (*ranchería* in Mexico), a common form of rural settlement in Latin America, is neither rural village nor typical dispersed settlement.

and adrift during the rest of the year. The poorest European peasant has a higher level of living than the landless peon or patch agriculturalist. Some immigrants find it difficult if not impossible to adjust to the new physical and social environment, but the majority soon feel at home and act as a leaven in society. They bring with them new skills, new attitudes, new techniques. They have proved to be good mechanics, machinists, and tractor and truck drivers; they do a lot of the work, both skilled and unskilled, connected with new construction everywhere. Many of them have settled in the cities and towns where in a few years they have established attractive stores, pharmacies, hotels, restaurants, and so on, especially in towns such as Barinas, Guanare, Acarigua, and Mérida. But they are also making their influence felt in the country. Foreigners have worked alongside Venezuelans in opening up the vast forested area in the Selva de Turén. They have become interested in the growing of rice. On the ranch of Don Tomás Rivas, near Ciudad Bolivia, two Italians who drive the tractors and do the work connected with the cultivation of rice have been given a 10 per cent interest in the crop as an incentive.

Cattle ranching and rice growing: a private project.—This investigation is concerned more with the activities of farmers and ranchers, who are largely independent of government sponsorship. A visit to the Rivas ranch, first seen by the senior writer in March and April 1929, made possible on-the-spot observations of changes wrought in ranching practices and agricultural techniques by an individual rancher. Don Tomás was born in Mérida and moved at the age of eight to Santa Bárbara de Zamora (now Barinas), where he worked as a peon for a number of years. After his father's death he was the main support of his mother and younger brothers and sisters. He gradually began to accumulate a little capital, with which he bought cattle from the plains to sell in the markets of the mountain towns and hamlets. By 1928 he had enough capital to buy the ranch, Caheta, where he has been in the cattle business ever since. When the senior writer visited the ranch in 1929, Don Tomás had about 1,500 cattle, many of which were killed each year by foot-and-mouth disease. His life on the llanos was a constant struggle with the elements. "La tierra es brava por que es brava la gente," he complained.

As a case in point, he explained that he holds 20,000 acres of land *por linderos* (according to natural boundaries) but only 15,000 acres *por escrituras* (according to his papers). The discrepancy reflects the insecurity of tenure common in many parts of Latin America. Indeed, at the time of the senior writer's visit in 1964, Don Tomás' son was away from the ranch looking after a lawsuit brought against his father regarding a piece of property he had bought from the plaintiff in 1931 for $2,000. It was alleged that the children of a first marriage had rights in this property which were not invalidated by the sale. It was all complicated, so much so that Don Tomás considered it the wiser course to settle the whole business out of court, at a cost of $9,000. Uncertainty of landownership often leads to confusion as to which lands belong to the federal government and which to private holders. Security of tenure would be a boon to landholders everywhere, for they would then have a personal interest in achieving maximum production.

Then the rancher recounted the natural hazards met in cattle raising. Unexpected and protracted periods of drought or rains may dry up the natural pastures or flood them under a foot or more of water over wide areas. Fortunately, the depredations of foot-and-mouth disease have been greatly reduced, as have those of the *nuche*, or *gusano de monte* (the larva of the warble fly, which lives under the skin of cattle until it matures and drops to the ground). Formerly, infestation with these larvae was so severe that cattle often died or lost a great deal of weight. Insect pests of all kinds are being controlled by the widespread use of DDT; animals are dipped frequently, stagnant ponds or swamps are being reduced in number, and containers around dwellings are no longer allowed to stand to collect water.

The herd on the Rivas ranch is being improved by crossing with zebu bulls. Cattle thus crossbred have a greater resistance to ticks, warbles, and horseflies, and to the midday heat. They are able to put on weight more rapidly than the native animals, even when pastures are poor in periods of drought. Indeed, native steers may be poor and emaciated while those with zebu blood, fortified with hybrid vigor, or heterosis, are sleek and fat, though both are grazing the same pasture.

The ranch house and the road leading to it are on a natural levee of the Acequia River. The levee, of sandy loam, stands a yard or so higher than the area on each side, where old stream channels and meander scars form temporary lakes or ponds, *esteros*, most of which do not survive the dry season. The low-lying, water-filled depressions are underlain by a heavy, compact, almost impermeable layer of the finest silt, and cattle pasture on the tender grasses that come up in them when the water has receded.

There has been a gradual trend toward planting artificial pasture, which will support more stock per unit of land and make it easier to tide cattle over the dry season. Don Tomás has experimented with artificial pastures for some time. He has found *gordura* grass (*Melinis minutiflora*) to do well in the Andean foothills and Front Ranges, but it does not survive burning. *Pará* grass (*Panicum purpurascens*) does best in the lower lying, poorly drained areas, such as former stream beds and meander scars. But he has found the best artificial pasture to be *pasto argentino*, or *jaragua* (*Hyparrhenia rufa*) [8] which survives the dry season and the annual burning. He has 1,250 acres of this grass, fenced, to cut for seed, and from this he expects to harvest about 40 pounds per acre, which would sell at 25 to 30 cents a pound.

Don Tomás is able to go into the business of growing rice without asking for government credit except for machinery. He already has 500 acres in rice and may plant more later. However, he hopes to be able to pay off the costs of machinery, seed, fertilizer, and labor within three years, make a reasonable profit, and then plant Argentine grass where he now grows rice. Rice growing is but a short-lived incident in his long-range plans for increased beef production. He expects that within five years his cattle will all be hybrids, with some proportion of zebu blood, and that as a result the value of his ranch will have just about doubled. His ranch cannot help but keep increasing in value, with improved pastures and herds and fields under rice. He already has 18 miles of fence around the rice fields and artificial pastures and along the boundary lines. A yearling steer sells for at least $50, a cow for breeding is worth $100, and a fine bull sells for $350. Don Tomás had recently sold a heifer of three-quarters zebu blood for $350. In telling of this, he recalled some of the changes that had taken place since he used to work with a yoke of oxen from three o'clock in the morning until nightfall for 15 cents a day.

8. Hiram Bingham, in *The Journal of an Expedition across Venezuela and Colombia, 1906–1907*, gives a vivid account of the leaven introduced into this area by an energetic Colombian, Don Francisco Parada Leal, originally from the mountain town of Sogamoso, who was a "most intelligent person." It was from him that the son of Don Tomás Rivas received a packet of seeds of the Argentine grass that has proved so valuable both to Don Tomás and to his fellow ranchers.

Don Tomás is well aware of the role of good wholesome food, and lots of it, in maintaining the health and efficiency of his workmen. The diet has certainly improved in the past forty years. There seems to be more emphasis on the protective foods, especially meat, eggs, and cheese. The use of fruits and vegetables is not yet as common as might be wished; for instance, the lemons from the several trees near the ranch house were all left to rot on the ground.

Each evening Don Tomás, seated on his veranda, watches his herd come in from the plains to spend the night near the ranch house. His face reflects an inner peace as he contemplates the stock. All his life he has toiled so that his children will inherit a strong herd on unencumbered land. He has a clear vision of what the ranch will be, either under his personal supervision, as now, or under that of his son, Trinidad.

The federal government continues to pump millions of dollars into a kind of agricultural "Operation Bootstrap" in Zulia, in the Amacuro Delta, in the Tuy Valley, as well as in the llanos. Rice production was a bonanza until the domestic market was saturated. But without an export subsidy, Venezuelan rice cannot compete in the world market with rice from low-cost countries such as Brazil and Ecuador. The domestic consumption of sugar continues to increase. Cuban capital was attracted even before the advent of Fidel Castro. The natural resources in the transition zone between the Andes and the great grassy plains are being utilized more intensively every year. Vast stretches of the grasslands are being fenced and support thriving herds of cattle with an increasing percentage of zebu blood. Cattle are more and more being taken to market by truck instead of on the hoof. Thousands of acres of dry rice (*secano*) are grown on the permeable, sandy soils at the foot of the Front Ranges, on land that only a few decades ago was almost completely valueless.

In a recent study, E. Willard Miller analyzes factors which have changed the status of Portuguesa and Barinas from a region with a low density of population possessing a primitive pioneer agricultural economy to a region with an expanding population and a developing commercial agricultural economy. He concludes his paper, based in large part on optimistic reports of the National Agrarian Institute, with words of cautious optimism: "Despite problems, which sometimes appear insurmountable, a commercial agricultural economy is evolving in the western llanos. The expanding production of rice, corn, sesame, and other commodities has contributed significantly to the national economy. The western llanos could become a prototype for other pioneer agricultural regions in Latin America."[9]

Las Majaguas: a government project.—In its endeavor to *sembrar el petroleo*, that is, to plow oil revenues into national industry and agriculture, the government of Venezuela has undertaken numerous projects aimed at total agricultural reform which, besides land distribution, includes irrigation, flood control, the provision of public health facilities, schools, transportation facilities, and marketing arrangements. Agricultural technicians will advise on all factors having to do with tropical soil management.

One such project now under way is located near Acarigua, a town of more than 30,000 inhabitants, founded by the Spaniards in 1647 on a site previously occupied by the Arawak Indians. It occupied a strategic position between the llanos and the coast, via the Barquisimeto-Yaracuy depression, at the same time that it was accessible to Valencia and Carácas by passable trails over which cattle from the grasslands were driven to market. By constructing dams on the Sarare and Cojedes rivers, some 80,000 acres of fertile land could be irrigated by gravity flow through irrigation cahals on the gently sloping piedmont alluvial plain. Roads, houses, schools, and community centers have been constructed.

At Las Majaguas, the goal is to raise the level of living by providing land and jobs. The rural proletariat of the nation is already crowding the land, underemployed, restless, migrating to the towns and urban centers where, without skills, it leads a precarious existence in growing slums. The government feels that the problem of rural displacement would be aggravated by consolidation of land into large farms and the adoption of modern mechanized farming methods. As an alternative, the project at Las Majaguas provides parcels of land, housing, and credits to those participants accepted into the scheme; they receive a salary the first year, at the same time that they are trained in modern agricultural techniques. After a year, a farmer takes over a parcel of land (25 acres if he goes into crop farming, 42 acres if he chooses to raise cattle). He enjoys the protection of commodity price support, and he has eight years in which to pay off the mortgage on his land. He and his family live

9. "Population Growth and Agricultural Developments in the Western Llanos of Venezuela: Problems and Prospects," p. 26.

in a *poblado central* made up of a dozen or more houses. Children go to the local school (four grades). A concrete-block house, pure drinking water, plumbing, and electricity are provided.

In 1966, significant amounts of corn, sesame, and safflower were raised at Las Majaguas, but 80 per cent of the cropland was used for rice culture. This crop, popular with the *parceleros*, is a good cash crop, for its yield is reliable and it enjoys government price support. There is, however, surplus production of rice in Venezuela, whose government must sell the excess at a loss on the world market. Hence, the authorities at Las Majaguas are trying to produce less rice, and to emphasize such crops as industrial seeds, corn, cotton, tobacco, beans, and fruits. Efforts at diversification have met certain obstacles, for the soils at Las Majaguas are excellent for rice culture. But the longer rice is produced on a given plot of land, the more difficult it is to grow other crops there. Rice culture is seen as a kind of blind alley by the authorities at Las Majaguas. In the effort to divert the parcelero from rice culture, by diversifying crops, the Las Majaguas management committee, which has ultimate authority as to what crops will be grown, is recommending the production of crops that do not have to compete on the world market. Attempts to grow cotton have not been economically successful. It cannot compete with cotton from tropical lands such as Costa Rica or Peru. But can the Venezuelan government continue to underwrite losses in a project aimed at raising levels of living of the rural poor? Efforts to operate general farming at Las Majaguas continue in the hope of producing crops that will pay their own way. An alternative would be to buy general commodities in the world market while devoting Venezuelan agriculture to large-scale mechanized plantation crops which would yield an economic return. But such a step does not solve the problem of rural under- and unemployment. This is especially the case in a country that is just beginning to industrialize.

As viewed by the modern city dweller, life in the tiny agglomeration of Las Majaguas is not attractive. A relentless sun blazes down on a dozen tiny houses, a water tower, a school, and a poorly stocked general store—all strung out along a dusty road. In 1964, 300 families were moved from the *ranchitos*, or slums, of Carácas to Las Majaguas with the hope that they would like it there. But once exposed to the animated life in a big city—with its television, neon lights, movies, and fiestas—people do not relish living in remote, coldly impersonal agglomerations where neither community nor blood relations act as a cohesive societal cement. Those in charge of Las Majaguas had been able to imbue the immigrants from Carácas with some of their own enthusiasm, but it was synthetic and turned out to be short lived. These city dwellers missed the excitement of big city life, even as lived in the slums, and they gradually drifted away. Within two years only one-third of this group was still in residence in Las Majaguas.

Most significantly, however, other migrants have come in, mostly from the subsistence plots along the rivers or from the tiny, remote caseríos, where underemployment is the rule. For these people Las Majaguas is a step up, a most attractive place in contrast to where they have been living. This is the kind of migrant who should be recruited for such a project, a person who has not been influenced by life, even squalid life, in a big city. It was hoped that by the end of 1968, 2,000 families will be in residence—there were 900 in mid–1966. All the dams are completed, as are most of the irrigation canals. Land-clearing projects are continuing, and most of the basic engineering work has been completed.

Las Majaguas should be viewed not as an isolated colonization project, lost in the llanos, but rather as a part of the total Venezuelan effort to achieve national equilibrium in industry and agriculture. Oil revenue is being used to build industrial complexes, manufacturing capacity is growing rapidly, and rural dwellers are leaving the land for the cities, although most of them do not have the skills necessary to compete in an urban environment. Further, modern methods of public health, coupled with a high birthrate, have made for phenomenal growth in population. Las Majaguas is a first step for unskilled rural dwellers—step migrants. It is a staging area where these untrained campesinos can begin to create for themselves in this modern society an economic niche from which, if they have the capacity, they may graduate to more sophisticated milieux. Las Majaguas may gradually have a very different orientation, but for the present it is performing a valuable way-station service.

A developing landscape: a look toward the future.—During the last several decades, the government of Venezuela has invested huge sums in the construction of highways. This network of highways has greatly facilitated spatial spread of the population, and the nation as a result is becoming a stronger, more cohesive political unit. The nation is particularly interested in securing its frontier zones, especially the one with its sister republic Colombia in the west. It is now possible to reach San Cristóbal del Táchira from Maracaibo or Carácas, either by the Pan American Highway north of the Andes and south of Lake Maracaibo or by the road along the llanos-Andes border southeast of the Andes. This latter highway, part of the proposed Marginal Highway (Carretera Marginal de la Selva) that will extend from Venezuela to Santa Cruz, Bolivia, now crosses the Colombian frontier on the Arauca River. One result of these developments is that San Cristóbal has become a regional center of great importance.

The rapidly growing urban population of San Cristóbal (estimated 1972 population, 160,000) is increasingly able to find employment in local industry, for that city has broken out of the boundaries that were stationary for so long; it has become a center of development of light industry that employs the cheaper labor from Colombia in manufacturing goods that successfully compete with those of Valencia and the metropolitan area of Carácas. The expansion of the sphere of influence of San Cristóbal is an important factor in consolidating the southwestern frontier zone of Venezuela.

A rapid trip to the llanos from San Cristóbal makes one aware of the enormous progress in productive capacity induced by highway construction to the south and east of the city. The road to the south first passes through a narrow valley, on the fertile floor of which sugarcane is grown; ground locally in small *trapiches*, a coarse brown sugar is produced for local use. Bricks are burned in huge kilns, using as fuel locally mined coal as well as the kindling that is a by-product of the many sawmills that use logs brought in from the llanos.

Once over the highest point on the highway, the road is squeezed in between the river and the mountain slopes; houses are strung along for miles in a ribbon settlement. Their front porches may contain a hodgepodge of items: fish nets, dried fish hanging from strings, bicycles, flower pots, sometimes even the family donkey.

At La Palmita one passes into a somewhat wider valley where the patch agriculturalist is evident on the mountain slopes, and where tobacco is produced on the rich alluvial valley floor; at one place, there is a small field of perhaps five acres where papayas are being produced commercially.

Before reaching Santo Domingo, on the Río Frío, the valley begins to open out, rich alluvial terraces are much in evidence, and patch agriculture gives way to cattle grazing. There are several large herds of white humped zebu and of others that resemble Santa Gertrudis.

From El Pinal to La Pedrera the road follows a terrace overlooking the Río Dorados, with the great plains extending into the distance. But this area is not natural grassland, as much of the llanos of Apure and Barinas seem to be. It was originally almost completely forested; a great number of huge stumps and tremendous dead trunks of trees are still standing, and in the distance virgin forest is still to be seen.

In other words, much of the area from Santo Domingo to Guacas, except that which is subject to annual inundation, has been cleared of dense forest and is now covered with planted pastures. This tremendous deforestation gives rise to a considerable lumbering industry, and numerous sawmills have been set up locally; trucks transport huge logs to mills around San Cristóbal.

At La Pedrera the road joins the highway that connects with Santa Bárbara, Barinas, and Acarigua, and from La Pedrera to Guacas the main industry is grazing. The ranches have a prosperous look. New model cars are seen in front of several of the large ranch houses. Dipping vats are a feature of most of the corrals and it is obvious that the cattle are not infested with warbles (nuche or gusanos).

The fact that there is no one at home in several of the ranch houses at which we stop does not imply that the owners do not spend much time there. It simply means that it is so easy to go to town. Most of them are probably absentee, but the easier it is for rural dwellers to go to town for the day, the easier it is to have urban amenities installed in the country. The more pleasant it is to live in the country, the more people will continue to live there instead of moving to town.

Twenty and thirty years ago steers were brought in from the llanos on foot; many were lost en route, and those that did arrive in San Cristóbal had lost much weight and had to be fattened up again in holding pastures. Indeed, much of the land just beyond the edge of town was used for precisely this purpose. All this has changed with the building of the road and the availability of truck service. Today a fairly large fleet of trucks is kept busy hauling fat steers to market; trips that used to take weeks are now made in a matter of hours, and the animals arrive at market in excellent condition. It is no longer necessary to produce bony, rangy, steers that can stand long treks to market. Now that it is possible to take steers to market by truck, it is profitable to introduce and produce pure blood beef cattle.

From Guasdualito to the border with Colombia on the Arauca River, the great grasslands are exploited by prosperous ranchers who have a ready and accessible market for their product. The building of highways has been accompanied by the construction of public schools and the introduction of public health measures. Significant signs of progress everywhere in the modern Venezuelan landscape are the public schools of the Ministry of Education and the water tanks and DDT signs of the Department of Health.

OVERVIEW

Especially during the past decade, the great wealth produced by the oil wells and iron ore mines of Venezuela has continued in an ever increasing proportion to be plowed back into agriculture and industry. Increased purchasing power in the hands of the consumer and the farmer, good roads on which the latter can move his produce to market, and a decreased "take" for the middleman have acted as stimuli to the producers of food. Generally, as purchasing power increases, economic exchange between regions becomes more active and varied. The construction of a national network of good roads, the establishment of industries, and price supports for agriculture decrease under- and unemployment. General economic growth in turn goes a long way toward creating a cohesive society with geographic, economic, and social mobility. Venezuela is achieving a more stable agricultural economy and a growing middle class; some of the more powerful of its cultured elite are now aware of their social responsibilities.

The changes effected in the cultural landscape of western Venezuela during the past twenty-five years have been phenomenal. Given a stable government, good roads, good land, an assured market for agricultural products, public schools, public health facilities, and other amenities in a defined area, rapid evolution of the economy follows. Population grows rapidly, by natural increase as well as by immigration. Under- and unemployment decrease as people are engaged at higher profits and wages in agriculture, industry, and services. The productivity of a population enjoying good health is higher than that of a disease- and parasite-ridden labor force, and with increasing productivity, levels and standards of living rise in an upward spiral.

Agricultural development along the llanos-Andes border has incorporated a significant sector of the country into the national economy and has raised the level of living of its inhabitants. Indeed, the higher level of living achieved by most members of Venezuelan society over the past twenty-five years has meant a national upsurge in the development of arts and crafts, of science, and of education at all levels.

REFERENCES: VENEZUELA

Codazzi, Agustín. "El camino de Barinas a los Andes." *Cultura Venezolana* 7, no. 55 (1924) :125–53.

Comité Coordinador del Sistema de Riego Cojedes-Sarare, Región de Las Majaguas. *El plan de Las Majaguas.* Caracas, 1966.

Crist, Raymond E. "Along the Llanos-Andes Border in Venezuela: Then and Now." *Geographical Review* 46, no. 2 (April 1956):187–208.

———. "Along the Llanos-Andes Border in Zamora, Venezuela." *Geographical Review* 22, no. 3 (July 1932):411–22.

———. *Étude geographique des llanos du Venezuela occidental.* Grenoble: Imprimerie Allier Père et Fils, 1937.

Gumilla, Joseph. *El Orinoco ilustrado: historia natural, civil y geográfica de este gran río.* Madrid, 1745.

Lovén, Sven. "The Orinoco in Old Indian Times." *Atti del XXII Congresso Internazionale degli Americanisti* (Rome, 1926) (1928), 2:711–25.

Miller, E. Willard. "Population Growth and Agricultural Developments in the Western Llanos of Venezuela: Problems and Prospects." *Revista Geográfica*, no. 69 (Dezembro 1968), pp. 7–27.

Vila, Marco-Aurelio. *Aspectos geográficos del Estado Portuguesa.* Caracas, 1954.

Vila, Pablo. "La iniciación de la ganadería llanera." *El Farol* 22, no. 194 (Mayo / Junio 1961):2–8.

3. Colombia

In what might be called the "Wild East" of the Republic of Colombia, there is a broad transition zone where low-lying, grass-covered plains, the *llanos*, and the great rain forests of the upper Amazon and its tributaries seem to break on the foothills of the towering Andes like waves on a rocky coast. This sector of Colombia has been of interest to geographers for many years. Pérez wrote over a century ago:

> What was there in the Europe beyond the Rhine in Caesar's time? A vast forest unknown to the Romans, but from which later issued a horde of barbarians who invaded and destroyed the eternal empire. Today in this same forest, now covered with rich and populous cities, kings and emperors who govern a population of 100,000,000 people, display their power.
>
> It is certain that within one or two centuries Colombia will have a very large population. Meanwhile the growing population of Pasto, Popayán, and Neiva will push across the Cordillera Orientale; it will fell the forests, open roads, found towns, and gradually penetrate the vast plains of the immense Amazon Basin.[1]

The scarcity of agricultural land in the mountain sectors of Colombia—indeed of Andean South America—has grown ever more acute, especially during the twentieth century. In those areas blanketed by volcanic ash, soils were rich and deep, the inhabitants were industrious, frugal, and prolific, and the ownership of land was the summum bonum. Land was rarely bought or sold, it was divided equally among numerous heirs each generation, with the result that plots became so small that they were uneconomical to

1. Felipe Pérez, *Jeografía física i política de los Estados Unidos de Colombia*, p. 441.

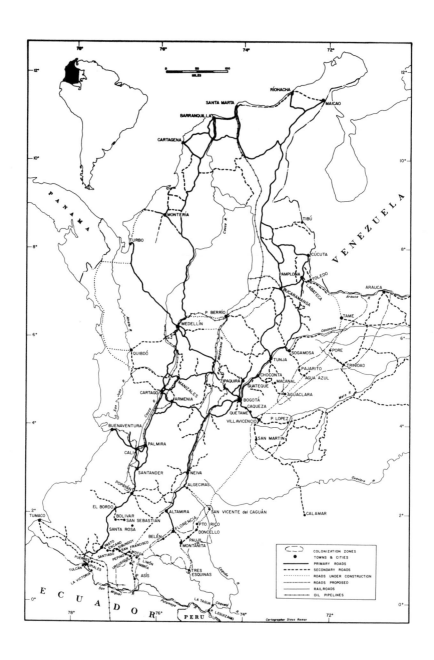

RÍOHACHA

SANTA MARTA

MAICAO

BARRANQUILLA

CARTAGENA

VENEZUELA

PANAMÁ

MONTERÍA

TIBÚ

TURBO

CÚCUTA

PAMPLONA

TOLEDO

ABREGA

ARAUCA

BUCARAMANGA

P. BERRÍO

TAME

MEDELLÍN

QUIBDÓ

SOGAMOSA

PORE

TUNJA

TRINIDAD

PAJARITO

CHOCONTA

AGUA AZUL

ZIPAQUIRÁ

GUATEQUE

MACANAL

MANIZALES

CARTAGO

BOGOTÁ

AGUACLARA

ARMENIA

CAQUEZA

QUETAME

BUENAVENTURA

VILLAVICENCIO

P. LOPEZ

PALMIRA

SAN MARTÍN

CALI

SANTANDER

NEIVA

ALGECIRAS

POPAYÁN

EL BORDO

ALTAMIRA

SAN VICENTE del CAGUÁN

CALAMAR

TUMACO

BOLIVAR

SAN SEBASTIAN

PTO RICO

SANTA ROSA

DONCELLO

BELÉN

FLORENCIA

PASTO

ENCANO

MONTAÑITA

SIBUNDOY

SAN FRANCISCO

PUERRES

SANTIAGO

PEPINO

TRES

ESQUINAS

TULCÁN

IPIALES

ORCUNGO

LIMÓN

UMBILA

LA VICTORIA

P. ASÍS

ECUADOR

PERU

LA TAGUA

P. LEGUIZAMO

San Miguel R.

Putumayo R.

Caguán R.

ECUADOR

	COLONIZATION ZONES
	TOWNS & CITIES
	PRIMARY ROADS
	SECONDARY ROADS
	ROADS UNDER CONSTRUCTION
	ROADS PROPOSED
	RAILROADS
	OIL PIPELINES

Cartographer Sieus Remar

MILES

work and not productive enough to support the owner and his family. Thus, in the mountainous sectors land hunger became acute.

In other parts of Colombia, both in hot country and in cold, much land formerly intensively cultivated has been incorporated into large estates devoted to cattle grazing. At the same time the intensive agriculturalists have had to move ever higher into the mountains onto the steeper, less fertile sectors, until even the poor areas were taken up. Then these people, face to face with hunger, were forced to migrate or perish. The great estates absorbed very few of these docile, submissive workers, and even those few at ridiculously low wages. Many of these uprooted workers sought employment in the mines or on the highways under construction in various parts of the country; still others were willing to venture into the virgin country to the east and south of the great wall of the Cordillera.

Although there are many passes across the Cordillera Oriental, in Colombia, the observations on which this chapter is based were made largely along those highways that are the most significant, actually or potentially, in giving access to these sectors of lowland eastern Colombia that are tributary to the Orinoco and to the Amazon. Field studies were also made along the mountain front itself, as well as on the great plains, or llanos.

THE BOGOTÁ-VILLAVICENCIO HIGHWAY

Climate.—Most readers are more vividly aware of climatic conditions if they know some details about day-to-day temperatures, rainfall, humidity, and winds than if they see "fossilized" weather on a climatic map. Hence some introductory remarks are in order on the elements of weather and climate in Villavicencio, a typical "gateway-to-the-llanos" town.

The rainfall at Villavicencio, 1,500 feet above sea level, is high, with an annual average of about 200 inches. It is fairly well distributed throughout the year, with higher than usual monthly averages from April through November. The evaporation rate is high and the runoff rapid, and at no time of the year does one feel any marked oppressive humidity. Temperatures at night are about 70° F. and the maximum day temperatures fluctuate between 86° and 93° F.[2] Thus, cool evenings and nights follow hot days in

2. Marston Bates, "Climate and Vegetation in the Villavicencio Region of Eastern Colombia," p. 570.

succession, and the annoyances considered by many to be synonymous with tropical climate are minimal.

Precipitation at Buena Vista, 4,000 feet above sea level but only
4 miles from Villavicencio, is 252 inches, or twice that received at
Puerto López, 45 miles east of Villavicencio, which is the head of
navigation on the Meta River.

From the Venezuelan frontier southward and westward to the
Macarena Massif (some 50 miles southwest of Villavicencio),
stretches of savanna alternate with densely forested areas. From the
Macarena Mountains to the border with Ecuador, the entire area
is forested. This steep-sided, block-fault mountain seems to lie in a
zone with a climate transitional between that of the Orinoco area,
where the wet and dry seasons are marked, and the Amazon region
in which abundant precipitation falls throughout the year; further,
although itself uninhabited and located in a sector where there are
at present no permanent settlements, impressive petroglyphs carved
in hard quartzite seem to show that the Macarena has not always
been unpeopled.

Soils.—The extremely sandy, permeable soils of many of the foothills and of the alluvial fans laid down by intermittent streams have
been used largely as open range for scrub cattle. Prospects for crop
production on such soils are poor, but low yields of dry rice (*secano*)
could probably be obtained. In general it would probably be best
left as rangeland on which improved pastures could be introduced.
It might be mentioned, however, that many of our concepts of
geography, acquired in middle latitudes, may be subject to re-
vision. Once tropical soils are intensively managed, when, for example, annual savanna fires are prevented, when the hard crust is
broken up by deep plowing, and when animal fertilizer, phosphates,
nitrates, lime, and trace elements, or micronutrients, are used where-
ever necessary, productivity will be bound to increase.

Usually just beyond the front ranges or foothills there is a zone
of predominantly light-textured soils, and the vegetation grades
from low rain forest to bunch grass interspersed with scattered brush
and small trees. These soils are generally of dark color to a depth
of a foot or more, and the water table seldom falls to more than 3
feet below the surface even in the dry season; these soils are cleared
and prepared for cultivation with relative ease. With good crop
adaptation and management these moderately fertile soils would be
very productive. At present, yuca, corn, and plantains are generally

very successful on the better types of this soil. Much of the rice cultivation around Villavicencio is on these deep soils, and any substantial expansion of rice production will probably be brought
about through mechanization and the introduction of chemical
fertilizer on this same soil type. Peanuts would probably do very
well on the better drained soils. Those phases of this soil type that
are light in texture and poorly drained have been largely used
for pasture on a rather empirical basis. If attention were paid to
improving both pastures and livestock, production per unit area
would surely be greatly increased. Sugarcane is grown, mainly for
local use. Yields are fair and replanting is usually done after three
or four years of ratooning. Scientists are working to develop a soil-
building crop adjusted to this climate, the use of which in a crop
rotation would certainly increase general productivity. Between
Villavicencio and Puerto López the extensive treeless sectors of
claypan soils, underlain by an impermeable layer, have proved to be
ideal for the production of paddy rice.

The deep, well-drained, medium-textured, fertile, alluvial soils
in heavy rain forests along the rivers are well adapted to the production of plantains, corn, yuca, vegetables, citrus fruits, and improved pasture for cattle. These soils of sandy loam have a pH content of 6.0 to 7.0 to a depth of 3 feet or so. At present, one of the
limiting factors in developing this kind of land for large-scale commercial agriculture would be the expense involved in clearing. However, the labor and time of the pioneer with a machete are his own,
so he does not count the cost. With reasonably good soil management this kind of land is extremely favorable for cultivated crops
for a period of years; even without the use of fertilizers it will not
deteriorate rapidly.

Political upheavals and violence of any kind may bring about a
marked increase in the number of subsistence or near-subsistence
farmers. The violence—la violencia— in Colombia during the past
two decades has had the effect of breaking up many formerly settled
communities, some of whose inhabitants migrated to the cities in
search of a livelihood and protection, while others fled to the unsettled areas in the mountains or in the eastern plains of the country.
One such refugee, M. Rodríguez, living some 10 miles up the Meta
River from Puerto López, was from the mountains of Tolima,
where he had barely been able to scratch out a living from his tiny
plot. Murders of farmers in his vicinity became so common that he

feared for his life and moved to town, but he had no skills and could find no way of making a living. He was finally able to get a ride in a cattle truck returning to Puerto López from Bogotá. From there he went upriver in a dugout canoe with his wife and children, and began to grow a crop of corn at the edge of the river. He is at present a subsistence farmer, to be sure, but one that might correctly be referred to as a subsistence farmer in transition, because as soon as there is a market and he can produce a surplus he will be interested in entering a money economy by supplying that market with surplus corn, a fattened hog, a few chickens, papayas, or cooking bananas. Rodríguez had a helper, a Huitoto Indian girl, who was learning Spanish and in general taking on the ways of the sedentary agriculturalist. Thus this was a case of a subsistence farmer in transition using the labor of an Indian girl in process of acculturation. Her children will probably be better adapted to hot country farming than either she or the Rodríguez family is at present.

The soft shales and limestones in the vicinity of Cáqueza, on the Bogotá-Villavicencio highway, make an excellent soil, on which a dense population lives in dispersed settlements. This area was originally peopled by settlers from mountain slopes higher up, and it still receives recruits from there in spite of the fact that this sector in turn, owing to population pressure, supplies recruits for the settling of the piedmont forest and of the llanos at lower elevations. The llanos-Andes border is thus the scene of step migration; the process whereby mountaineers adjust to life in tropical lowlands may take a generation or more. In somewhat the same manner Yankees migrated from New England at the same time that French Canadians migrated to New England, for living conditions that seemed grim to Yankees seemed better to French Canadians.

For many centuries the vast grassy plains of Colombia, like those of Venezuela, have been ideal for the extensive grazing of cattle. However, with the construction of the Villavicencio-Bogotá motor road, intensification of agriculture is possible over large areas, rice is being grown as a cash crop, and land values are increasing. Rice production for the local market began during World War I when there was an influx of immigrants, mainly from Cáqueza and Quetame where population pressure had built up. During the twenties, there was vigorous trade between Villavicencio, Cáqueza, and Bogotá, in spite of the appalling state of the mule trail. The highway between these towns—the result rather than the cause of settlement—was completed between the years 1932 and 1936 and was later extended to Puerto López on the Meta River. With its completion there was a second wave of immigration, and rice became an increasingly important crop when it could be sent by truck to the Bogotá market at a handsome profit. The immigrants spread over the area of fine-textured alluvial soils between the Guatiquía and Guayuriba rivers. Here they grow dry rice, mostly on plots from 5 to 10 acres in size. A few farmers cultivate from 100 to 250 acres. The crop is harvested and sacked by hand, then transported by pack mule to one of the rice mills in Villavicencio. Farmers' harvests vary in size from one or two muleloads to as many as 150. In the mill the crop is dried, threshed, hulled, and sacked. Then it is piled neatly on a platform where it is tested by buyers, loaded on trucks, and shipped to Bogotá.

A third wave of immigrants has been arriving in the Villavicencio area since the political disturbances between 1950 and 1953. Most of these recent settlers are from Tolima and Caldas. It is indeed fortunate that this third wave of immigrants, and the second wave to some extent, are able to enjoy the advantages of certain modern public health measures. A vigorous health campaign has virtually eliminated malaria, once the scourge of this fertile area. To appreciate the significance of this change one has but to read the accounts of travelers a generation or two ago: "Villavicencio is no place for persons of nervous temperament, nor are the people whom one begins to meet a day before the town is reached (over the trail from Bogotá) pleasant to look at, with their lemon-tinted, gaunt, emaciated faces and hands of horribly lethal thinness."[3]

Travel in this sector even today is not without its hazards. Even the main road to the southwest, between Villavicencio and San Martín, is graveled only part way. The forest has been cut away and corn, yuca, plantains, and rice are grown for the Bogotá market. The bridge for heavy traffic across the Humadea River has been under construction for years. A family, originally from Tolima, who had settled in good faith on what they understood was state-owned land (terrenos baldíos), on which they had built a clapboard-roofed house and cleared plots for their cash crops, were at the time visited engaged in a dispute with a person from San Mar-

3. Hamilton Rice, "Further Explorations in the Northwest Amazon Basin," p. 140.

tín who claims that the land legally belongs to him, and who has a paper (*escritura*) to substantiate his claims. Of course, he had never done anything himself that would give the land value; he merely showed up to take advantage of the fruits of the labors of others. The woman of the house is the mother of ten children, three of whom are grown and work their own plots of land in this sector. All her children are living. The public health factor is extremely important. Whereas a generation or so ago at least half of the children would have died in infancy, now a much higher percentage lives to maturity. And the child-bearing days of this particular woman are probably not over—as the local idiom has it, she still has "la casa ardiendo"—roughly equivalent to "still going strong."

Many of the mountaineers who came into this area to work as laborers when the highway was under construction cleared land and settled on it after the work was completed. Many of them are now planting coffee and cacao, which will make them a tidy income later. They grow rice, corn, and yuca as subsistence crops; any surplus finds a ready market.

San Martín was founded by the Jesuits as a mission in the seventeenth century, yet in 1912 it consisted only of "rambling houses and a half-completed church built around an enormous plaza."[4] But there was good reason why the village did not prosper. At that time, Hamilton Rice, a medical doctor, found the tertian form of the malarial parasite, sometimes in conjunction with the subtertian, in all the 250 cases of adults and children whose blood he examined. His picture of the tiny struggling village was indeed pessimistic:

> San Martin, with its innumerable puddles, ditches, and foul house yards is a prolific breeding ground [of the malarial mosquito], and, owing also to the existence there of an especially virulent form of malaria which the rubber-collectors and muleteers bring in from the adjoining swamp district, the town has a notoriously and deservedly bad reputation. The town carpenter, whose most lucrative business is the making of coffins, and who thus serves as the only available bureau of vital statistics, assured me he made from two to three a week, but added, with a grim smile, that many have no pesos with which to pay and are buried without boxes.[5]

4. Ibid., p. 142.
5. Ibid.

San Martín has experienced rapid growth in the past generation. It would not be recognized by those who saw it thirty years ago. The best selling item in the large drugstore is face cream, closely followed in importance by nail polish and lipstick! Safety razor blades are sold at the rate of slightly over 3,000 a month. Many migrants pass through here on their way south and west, to areas as yet unsettled, particularly around Boca de Monte, eight miles south of San Martín. This village, only a few years ago a cluster of palm thatch huts literally at the edge of the forest, as the name implies, is now a thriving center, owing largely to the arrival of some 300 people from Armenia (Quindio). These settlers told of the grim struggle for existence in their former locale, where land is scarce and hopelessly subdivided into plots so small as to be uneconomical, and where wages are pitifully low; they have brought with them their seasoned habits of frugality and hard work, and have carved farmsteads out of the public lands on which they grow corn, yuca, and plantains for home use and rice for the market. As the edge of the forest recedes the name Boca de Monte will have a significance more historical than actual.

The Ariari River southwest of Villavicencio is the boundary line between conservatives and liberals, who have a traditional and deadly hatred of each other. To quote a normally mild-mannered bus companion, "It is necessary to kill a lot of people, but those who should be killed are the ones who are ordering people killed." The conservatives on the left bank have the road, but the liberals on the other side have the good land. These enemies are trying to cooperate enough to put a cable across the river, which can be used by both factions. Perhaps if the federal government built a road and a bridge, the political hatred, reminiscent of the religious intolerance and intervillage feuds of the Near East, would die down somewhat. The serious workers do want peace and work, rather than fighting and revolutionary activity. Most Colombians have rejoiced as recent political regimes have captured outlaws, quelled fratricidal strife, and emphasized peaceful pursuits for all. There were some who had acquired the habit of stealing rather than working during the years of civil strife, but fortunately they have rapidly returned to hard work.

Villavicencio, a city of 60,000 (1970), continues to grow, vertically as well as horizontally; it now contains several buildings with ten or more storeys. Each year the highway network is pushed

Villavicencio in 1941, a tiny frontier settlement, "east of the Andes and west of nowhere."

Villavicencio in 1970, a growing commercial center connected by a good road to the highland market. Its rich hinterland produces rice, cotton, and blooded cattle.

farther and farther out on the plains. The production of rice and blooded cattle continues to increase in the hinterland of this growing center. A crop that has assumed importance only recently is cotton, transported in enormous diesel trucks to the growing market in Bogotá. The growth and development of Villavicencio and its environs over the past thirty years is little short of amazing.

The vast, roughly triangular area which has Puerto López, Villavicencio, and San Martín as its apices, originally forested in large part, has been converted in many sectors by shifting cultivation and burning into savanna and partially improved grasslands. Great changes have taken place during the past three decades, induced in large part by the completion of the road from Bogotá to Villavicencio. In 1941 along the dirt road between Villavicencio and Puerto López there was perhaps a rangy steer for every 20 to 30 acres in tough, wiry natural grasses. By 1972 this whole area, largely sandy loam and deposits of fertile alluvial silt, had had its carrying capacity for cattle increased ten- to twentyfold; large herds of sleek, fat Charolais steers now graze on intensively managed pastures. They are trucked to market in a matter of hours, thus arriving in prime condition. Further, vast acreages, on which the very latest agricultural techniques are employed, are devoted to the production of cotton for the Bogotá mills. Thousands of acres are in rice that is hulled in modern mills. The savanna soils in particular were considered almost worthless thirty years ago, except for the most extensive form of grazing with a very low carrying capacity. Modern intensive management and the application of efficient technology in all its aspects have given these soils value, to produce blooded stock, rice, or cotton. In occupying this sector, modern man has created a productive, ecologically sound cultural landscape.

THE CHOCONTÁ-AGUACLARA HIGHWAY

The trail from Aguaclara, at the edge of the llanos, to Chocontá, in the highlands, via Santa María, Somandoco, and Guateque, was used for centuries for driving cattle from the hot country to the markets in the highlands; trucks loaded with cattle from the llanos roll over this former trail, now widened and graveled for all-weather wheeled traffic. At present, semiferal steers are the most important cargo passing through Aguaclara from the llanos; an extension of the highways south and east from this gateway-to-the-llanos town will open up this part of the great plains to the type of large-scale agriculture already found in the sphere of influence of the thriving metropolis of Villavicencio, where rice, cotton, and blooded cattle on artificial pastures are the significant products.

This highway has brought the densely populated highlands of the upper valleys of the Batá and its tributaries closer to the market of Bogotá. The result has been an intensification of agriculture in an area of dispersed settlement and minifundia. For example, previously unused boundaries between fields, a yard or so wide, are now planted in soilage grasses for stall feeding of milk cows; milk and cheese are produced for local or Bogotá markets. The animal fertilizer is used to increase the production of crops in the tiny fields—corn, beans, lentils, squash, and so on. Citrus fruits are much more important now that they are within easy reach of a large growing market. In general, the rural population is much better off now that it is more closely tied to Bogotá. Household industries such as needlework, basket-weaving, and the making of handbags are also thriving.

Another boon to this area will be the dual-purpose dam to be built at the narrow gorge of the Batá River near Macanal; this construction will give great value to rugged terrain that up to now has been almost completely uninhabited.

The Neiva-Florencia Highway

During the war with Peru in 1932, when the most deadly enemy proved to be the diseases so often associated with the tropics, Colombian Amazonia assumed great importance for the nation. The national government hastily planned roads into a vast tropical area that had been neglected so long that there were serious differences of opinion as to where the international boundary line should be drawn. The road to Florencia was originally planned to run from Neiva to La Tagua on the Caquetá River, via Florencia and Tres Esquinas, the latter town at the junction of the Caquetá and Orteguaza rivers.

Florencia.—In the last decade of the past century, gatherers of wild rubber and quinine made clearings along the Orteguaza and Hacha rivers, and they planted yuca, corn, and plantains. Shortly after, a clearing was made for the planting of cane, and a still was set up for distilling raw rum. The first settlement was called La Perdiz, but the name was soon changed to Florencia. Then depression struck the wild-rubber and quinine industries and very shortly all that remained of Florencia was the name.

The town of Florencia was officially founded in 1908 when thirty-seven of the principal settlers agreed to construct their houses in accordance with a map drawn up by the Capuchin priest, Father Fidel de Montclar.

The highway reached Florencia from Altamira in 1932, at the time of the war with Peru. The construction of the road meant that this potentially rich area became economically tributary to a high-land hinterland from which it attracted immigrants and to which it could ship its products. In this instance the highway was the cause rather than the result of settlement—the reverse of the situation in the Bogotá-Villavicencio sector.

The people who actually settle on the land are the advance columns who make it possible for the bridgeheads along the piedmont to survive. The highways and rivers are the arteries along which people flow in response to demographic pressure. The more one sees of active, voluntary colonization, the less faith one can have in settlement projects entirely sponsored by the government. Government agents, representatives, or inspectors are little interested in going to zones in which actual pioneering is taking place. They want to "inspect" areas that are already equipped with airstrips, hotels or guest houses, and other modern conveniences. In several places it was pointed out that "no one from the government ever comes out here. A man from Bogotá might spend the day in Florencia between planes, but *we* never see him!" The bus drivers were amazed that anyone should want to go to Montañita—the end of the line!

In the environs of Florencia, within a radius of eight to ten miles, the forest has been cleared away and permanent pastures established. This area has been settled long enough so that trees and stumps have all completely decayed.

Soils.—The soils between Florencia and Montañita, in the areas with almost no gradient as well as on the slopes of the low hills, are fine textured but fairly well drained. Those southwest of town, on the road to Belém, are poorly drained. Ponds of water, some small, others acres in extent, stand in the pastures for days after each rain. They dry up only when there is a week or so without rain.

Montañita.—Montañita itself, twenty miles southeast of Florencia, is in an area of rapid colonization. It was just a group of houses (*caserío*) until 1940 when a central square, or plaza, was laid out where meat and other products were brought in for sale. Sr. Muñoz is a typical inhabitant. He settled on a piece of land half a mile from Montañita when he came to this sector in 1922. The whole area was in forest at that time and tied to the outside by a very poor mule trail. He worked on the telegraph line for four years while clearing land for pastures and food crops. Now he has some 750 acres cleared—200 where he lives and 550 on the trail to the village of Puerto Rico. He is self-sufficient as far as basic foodstuffs are concerned: he has three acres of plantains, one acre of yuca, and one-half acre of sugarcane. The cane continues to produce enough sweet juice each year for household use, although it has not been replanted in thirty years. The soil is good, but not as good as in Huila. It is especially poor in calcium and deficient in nitrates and phosphates. Fertilizers would be a great boon, but chemical fertilizers are too expensive and animal fertilizer is not collected. The stall feeding of soilage crops would produce animal fertilizer that would be an important factor in the rational management of cleared but unoccupied land. Citrus fruits would do well, but no one plants or tends them systematically. Vegetables are little planted or used. There is plenty of meat available, a little milk, but practically no cheese.

The son-in-law of the rancher, Sr. Díaz, was worried about the generally inadequate diet and its relationship to fatal diseases, such as malaria or *paludismo* (almost any fever goes under this name), and to tropical anemia, caused in large part by hookworm infestation. Díaz himself had had yellow fever and was very near death, but recovered—thanks, he felt, to the fact that he had always had a fairly adequate diet. He hoped that some kind of extension service, which would bring farmers advice on agriculture and on diet and health, would be inaugurated by the federal government, but he was not too hopeful. He did mention a case of the unexpected consequences that can come from man's interference with the natural environment. In the days of banana-patch plumbing, the well-drained area of Montañita and vicinity was relatively free of mosquitoes. However, the construction of privies has meant the creation of stagnant pools of water in which mosquitoes find an ideal breeding place. The result was a plague of these pests and a high incidence of malaria. In spite of this hazard, however, everyone seemed happy to be in this pleasant spot. "The climate in Huila may be more salubrious, but here it is easier to make a living," commented the head of the house. And those born and brought up in this part of Colombia are in love with everything about it and have no desire to go anywhere else. The oldest son had returned to Huila for his bride, but he had no desire to stay there. Large families are the rule. The man of the house told me of the wonderful remedies to be found in the forest, particularly *quina* (wild quinine) for a "touch of fever," *mochilita* for constipation, or *higuerón* for a bilious attack.

The influence of a highway is felt over a wide zone. For example, the small village of Puerto Rico, northeast of Montañita, and San Vincente del Cagúan, a day's horseback ride beyond, both formerly shipped their products by mule train across the mountains to Algeciras and Neiva. However, with the extension of the road from Florencia to Montañita, the commercial activity of Puerto Rico is oriented toward the end of the truck route at Montañita. The produce from San Vicente, however, still moves over the mountains by muleback to Algeciras.

Large estates and small clearings.—Southeast of Florencia at the confluence of the Orteguaza and Hacha rivers, the extremely wealthy Lara family bought an estate, once the road had reached Florencia, of some 37,500 acres of land on which several thousand head of steers were soon grazing. They got government land cheap, land tied to a well-populated hinterland by a fairly good road. The investment has continued to increase in value.

By 1966 the Laralandia operation had grown tremendously. It then contained some 187,500 acres of pasture on which 40,000 head of cattle grazed—the largest cattle ranch in Colombia. The pastures that were deforested and burned in 1938 are still in use today; pastures planted after the slash-and-burn operation are able to thrive indefinitely, as long as they are intensively managed. There is still the problem of getting the product to market. The logical development, as long as the main consuming centers are far away, would be to slaughter the animals locally and ship out the frozen meats by plane or refrigerator truck. In time, as population in the Oriente builds up, there will of course be a growing local market for meat.

Settlers from downriver bring their produce in great dugout canoes, or *bongos*, to Puerto Lara. Bags of yuca, corn, rice, and plantains, fattened hogs, chickens, exotic birds, sewing machines,

suitcases, and household effects are here transferred from the dugouts to trucks for shipment to Florencia, Neiva, or even Bogotá.
Some huge canoes are used for the transportation of enormous
planks of mahogany and tropical cedar. The dugouts are no longer
paddled by hand. Almost every one of them has an outboard motor
attached to it, and this means a relatively cheap and rapid means
of transport for goods and passengers. The head of canoe navigation on these rivers running from the eastern Andes into the llanos
is now, thanks to the internal combustion motor, easily reached by
people living fifty miles or more out on the plains. When canoes
had to be paddled by hand the settler had to live within ten or
fifteen miles of the head of navigation. One settler on the Río Pescado, twenty-five airline miles away, brought two immense hogs,
fattened on corn and yuca, to be loaded on the truck and marketed
in Florencia. It would have been impossible to transport them by
dugout canoe when the trip was measured in days instead of hours.
The zone of influence, or the radius of attraction, for each head of
navigation is thus extended downstream from a maximum of ten
to fifteen miles, formerly, to a distance of fifty miles or even more.
About 80 per cent of the settlers who are establishing their beach-
head farms on the rich *vega*, or natural levee, land along the rivers
are from Huila.

Food crops and village trading techniques.—The frontiersman in
the Andean foothills plants a patch of yuca, corn, or plantains, depending on the local climatic and edaphic conditions and on the
starch to which he has always been accustomed. However, the
favorite starch food for the dweller of the llanos is the topocho
(*Musa paradisiaca* L.), a small eating and cooking banana that is
resistant to high winds, drought, and lack of care. Once a topocho
patch is started it continues to bear for years; it is the staff of life
for the *llanero*. After it has been grated and dried in the sun, it is
used in making fecula for feeding small children; green or ripe it
is used at every meal—boiled, baked, roasted, or fried. The topocho
is also used as feed for chickens, hogs, work animals, and milk cows.
The leaves are used as wrapping paper in an area where that commodity does not exist. Rice and corn are frequently planted between
the rows. When harvested, the rice is kept in sacks in the loft, the
ears of corn are tied in pairs by the husk and hung near the roof
over the open kitchen fire, where it dries quickly; the smoke discourages weevils.

In the tiny stores on the streets of Florencia nearest the public market an infinitesimal amount of goods is sold each day—possibly not more than five pesos' worth. However, it is impossible to get at the real economic life of most storekeepers in terms of statistics. Books are simply not kept. Further, urban and rural functions are so tightly interwoven that it is next to impossible to unravel the individual strands. For instance, María Vermeo has a plot of twenty-five acres ("more or less") of land two miles west of Florencia. She raises corn, plantains, yuca, rice, and sugarcane, and grinds her cane and makes crude sugar in a primitive *trapiche*, or mill. She also has ten milk cows. Two of her sons have a tiny store on the plaza where they buy, sell, and trade chickens, hogs, eggs, plantains, or anything that comes along. They take one meal a day at the Tolima Hotel, owned by a cousin, to which their mother purveys firewood, milk, crude brown lump sugar, and cooking bananas. Hogs on Doña María's farm are fattened on the slops from the hotel. But statistics of any kind are lacking wherewith to analyze the economic lives of these people, most of whose activities cannot be tabulated by computer.

Some 80 to 90 per cent of rural Latin Americans live what are to them satisfactory lives, completely beyond the realm of statistics. From the point of view of classical economic theory, they do not exist at all, a fact that adds zest to the study of man's incumbency on the earth in that whole vast cultural area.

Forest settlements.—On the weekly flight from Florencia to the frontier military post of Puerto Leguízamo on the Putumayo River, the only intervening stop is at Tres Esquinas where the Río Orteguaza joins the Caquetá. Colonists have penetrated the heavy forest on a wide front south and east of Florencia as far as the point where the Río Pescado empties into the Orteguaza. From there on to the Putumayo one flies over continuous treescape with a totally un-lived-in aspect. Tres Esquinas, Puerto Leguízamo, and La Tagua on the Caquetá are typical of settlements made for strategic purposes along rivers. The riverbank is cleared for a half mile or so on either side of the settlement, but only a few hundred yards behind the settlement the dense forest swallows up a trail or a road. Much of the land lying unused in the llanos of Colombia could be put into the production of African oil palms, but this is a crop that requires a large capital outlay and long-term investment; hence oil palm production cannot be undertaken by the small-scale farmer, whose capital is often only a willingness to work hard. Such settlements have no hinterland and contrast sharply with the settlements at the foot of the mountains, such as Florencia, Mocoa, or Villavicencio that do have hinterlands and are tied to them by a highway. For even a poor road is better than no road at all. Landslides can and do block passenger and truck traffic for days at a time. However, the caravans of cars and trucks thus blocked do eventually get through, even in the rainy season, although truck drivers may have to help road workers drive bulldozers and bus passengers may have to help push the bus or shovel earth.

The Colombian Air Force, the Satena (Servicio de Aeronavegación para Territorios Nacionales) line, is providing settlers in the remote sectors of the llanos with a lifeline to market by charging passengers only half the price charged by commercial airlines—which in any case do not serve much of the backlands. A typical example of how colonization can be supplemented by the plane was seen at the Tres Esquinas air base. The commander of the base started building a seventy-mile road to Florencia and gave potential settlers part-time jobs on the air base or the road to provide an income while they cleared their land claims and put in a crop of corn. There was a thriving market for the corn at the air base as well as in the settlements along the Caquetá River. As early as 1964 farmers were air-freighting two or three tons of beef to Bogotá each week from the cattle they had bought on government loans.

The following paragraphs by Professor Eidt show that progress in colonization in eastern Colombia continues steadily:

> Periodic civil disturbances have caused long delays in filling up the land and an extraordinary preoccupation with strictly domestic adjustments to settlement. The most recent clash between Liberals and Conservatives, starting in 1946, resulted in the displacement of so many tens of thousands of people that the government began to consider seriously the possibility of colonization with refugees on empty federal lands, or *baldíos*. In 1956 the legal machinery for such colonization was placed in the hands of the Caja de Crédito Agrario. Field activities were delayed until December, 1959, when the Caja established six pioneer settlement zones for Colombian citizens between the ages of twenty-one and fifty-five in which holdings averaged fifty hectares per family. These settlement zones, in order of importance, are Caquetá, Ariari, and Sarare on the east side of

the Cordillera Oriental, and El Lebrija, Carare, and Galilea
on the west side. By 1967, titles had been granted to about 4000
families, and probably 40,000–50,000 other families have staked
out their own small holdings on which they raise sugarcane,
rice, maize, and cattle near government roads.

Of all the new pioneer settlement zones, Caquetá, lying south
and east of Florencia, is the most promising. It has been the
object of detailed investigation, which has been reported in two
recent publications (Victor Daniel Bonilla: Caquetá 1: El des-
pertar de la selva, *Tierra*, No. 2, Bogotá, Oct.–Dec., 1966; and
"Proyecto Caquetá No. 1 Os Saluda" [Instituto Colombiano de
la Reforma Agraria, Bogotá, 1966]). Both studies suggest numerous reasons for the mounting interest in the improvement
of Colombia's food supply and land distribution by means of
pioneer settlement. Colonists on relatively small holdings in
the Caquetá area harvested more than 10,000 hectares of rice
in 1966 at an estimated value of 32 million pesos, had by that
date imported 18,000 head of certified beef cattle, and had managed to bring to 36,000 hectares the amount of land under
title. Moreover, the area is on the verge of producing vegetable
oil from 835 hectares of African oil palm (1235 hectares were
expected by the end of 1967) at one assembled factory, and at
two additional plants destined for completion by 1969. One
million rubber trees are currently being planted; already they
occupy some 800 hectares.

The Caquetá area, which is now under the direction of the
Instituto Colombiano de la Reforma Agraria [Colombian Institute of Agrarian Reform] (INCORA), consists of four settlements, Maguaré, Valparaíso, La Mono, and Tres Esquinas, expanding toward one another across a hilly, tropical rain-forest
region. In each of these nuclei different colonization problems
have been encountered, and much has been learned that will
be applied to future pioneer centers already in the field planning stage.

Since most Caquetá colonists are displaced persons with little
or no experience, it has been found impractical to issue seeds
for valuable perennials such as African oil palm and rubber
because of the long wait until harvest time. Instead, INCORA
now plants 100-hectare plantations of these crops, cares for
them until they are nearly mature, and then subdivides the
plantations into 10-hectare plots, which are issued with title
to pioneers. From the moment harvests are in sight the individual settler is willing to give proper attention to his plot

while still receiving technical assistance and training from INCORA.

A hexagonal settlement form introduced at Valparaíso in the hope of producing more efficient expansion and utilization of space has failed because too many of the holdings lack water and are isolated from the road leading into the area. Funds for necessary radial tie roads have never been advanced. However, these problems can be overcome by the use of long parallel lots extending on each side of *trochas*, or inexpensive forest-cut trails. These holdings could have one end fronting a river or stream and the other the trocha that connects with the nearest market road. No tie roads are then necessary. This form of settlement has already been employed successfully at La Mono.

The enthusiasm generated by modest but increasing government assistance in the Caquetá region has attracted an estimated twenty thousand families to the area, only 15 percent of whom are supported by INCORA. All others are *colonos espontaneos*, or squatters, who, under Colombian law, can initiate title proceedings because this is baldío land. As a consequence, the government has not been able to extend appropriate settlement forms even in the areas for which they were originally planned. An important effect has been the surveying of subsequent lots according to the crude boundaries demarcated by spontaneous pioneers. Since the pioneers themselves are wise enough to settle where fresh water is available, this has proved a satisfactory solution for the moment, though field investigations reveal a tendency toward increased isolation of settlers as more arrive and are forced deeper into the selva beyond connecting roads. Sometimes this tendency is reversed and results in excessive subdivision of the more accessible areas, so that clusters of *minifundium* holdings occur in rural parts of the selva. Because there is not enough money for road building, the solution to this serious problem has to await better times, the assistance of armed-service road-construction battalions of the type already experimenting in Tres Esquinas, or the formation of roadbuilding cooperatives among colonists. Such cooperatives have been successfully applied at Maguaré and La Mono and were initiated at Valparaíso with INCORA help in July, 1967.

Where towns have not been planned, they are insisted upon by settlers. Three new towns—Doncello (about 3000 inhabitants), Puerto Rico (2000), and Paujil (1000)—have arisen in the selva since colonization began, and provide schools, clinics, stores, and recreational facilities, but they are considered too remote by many forest pioneers. Thus additional urban settlements are built at great expense by the colonists but sometimes at such poor sites that no expansion is possible and slum areas with little hope for civic improvement are quickly produced. This has occurred at Maguaré, and colonists are now planning another such center at La Mono against INCORA wishes. INCORA officials have learned that isolation is intensely felt in the selva even within short distances of civilization, and they recognize the need to include more urban centers in future planning.

In spite of serious problems, pioneer settlement in the Caquetá region has produced sufficiently favorable results that substantial federal financial assistance will probably continue during the next several years. The enthusiasm for planned pioneer settlement generated by Peruvian President Belaúnde Terry along his *Carretera Marginal de la Selva* east of the Andes has stimulated Colombians to refer to the new road from Maguaré to Florencia and La Mono, part of which has been paved, as a section of the "marginal highway" program. This is typical of the spirit encountered in the recently opened frontier region, which now attracts an estimated average of fifty pioneer families every month.[6]

In conclusion, it should be pointed out that this whole thriving development is based on a foundation of pre-existing infrastructure, such as the road to Florencia and, more recently, beyond to Montañita, Belém, and other points, and the long established air service to Tres Esquinas. Such factors, plus the heavy investments of the Lara brothers in their huge and prosperous ranching operations, help to create markets that greatly facilitate the development of such projects as those at Caquetá. Thus pre-existing roads, plus air service, are basic factors in achieving successful development that in turn lend support to, or snowball into, other successful ventures and developments, in an upward spiral.

According to an item in a recent issue of *Colombia Today*,[7] the Caquetá project already contains 3,500 individual farms, averaging 250 acres in size, and over 100,000 head of cattle, mostly Brahman. Transportation facilities on land, on the rivers, and in

6. Robert C. Eidt, "Pioneer Settlement in Colombia."
7. Vol. 7, no. 10 (1972) .

the air are being improved, and educational and health services are being made available to the 300,000 people now living in this general area, three times the number living there seven years ago.

The Colombian Institute of Agrarian Reform in the early part of 1969 announced plans to invest $40 million in the settlement of 2,200 farmers and their families on virgin lands in the Sarare and Ariari zones of the eastern plains. Some 350 miles of new road will be built to relocate these families on holdings ranging in size from 125 to 400 acres, on a total of 235,000 acres. Under this program of INCORA, supported by a $10.8 million loan from the International Development Bank, technical assistance to settlers will be provided and schools, medical care centers, and other social welfare facilities will be established.

THE SOGAMOSO–AGUA AZUL HIGHWAY

A highway is built and is used for two-way traffic. This is exemplified well in the area south and east of Sogamoso, a prosperous urban center set in a valley worked by thousands of industrious small-plot agriculturalists. The highway connecting this mountain center to the llanos crosses the high, cold *páramo* country around Laguna de Tota, where the inhabitants earn the barest of livings by grazing sheep on the bleak mountain sides or by growing tiny patches of potatoes. Only very gradually has this hard-working population begun to seep over the mountains to the llanos, along the precipitous trail used for walking rangy steers from the great plains to market. The road was a boon to the area when completed in 1948; settlers came in greater numbers, army posts were established in Pajarito and in Agua Azul, and what had formerly been almost exclusively a cattle trail became a busy highway with two-way traffic. Then came the civil disturbances. Rival factions engaged in indiscriminate killing. Many people on both sides lost their lives, many more took to the wilder, more rugged terrain and waited for the storm to blow over, but an even greater number very early in the struggle fled to the comparative security of the large cities by using the highway. Thus the area was effectively drained of a great number of its inhabitants. Only since the middle fifties have they begun to come back.

To be sure, many of the settlers left the mountains for the eastern frontier zone for social and political rather than purely economic reasons. They sought a new world in which to enjoy freedom from societal restraints rather than a geographic frontier in which to work out their economic freedom. Hence their social as well as their cultural heritage made them poor pioneers in virgin, unsettled territory. Much of the revolutionary, anti–central government discontent in the eastern llanos during the years 1950–53 was due to the leaven of these uprooted malcontents.

A Colombian pioneer.—All over the world there seems to be a rural exodus, a kind of tidal wave of human beings leaving the land for urban agglomerations, large or small, that grow by accretion. However, a reversal of this process—on a small scale, to be sure—seems to be taking place in various parts of Colombia, particularly in the transition belt between the vast plains of alluvial deposition and the massive Andean wall. Many of the settlers entering this zone have been pushed off the land, either from large estates or from plots too small to support a family. However, a large part of this wave of migrants is made up of former urban dwellers, men who have made their living as artisans or industrial workers. It can become so difficult to make a living in urban agglomerations that they cease to grow by accretion—indeed they may, and do, supply the recruits for pioneer fringe settlements. The pioneer settlers are to a great extent mountaineers, rural or urban, who hail from those regions of cold, rugged terrain that are feeling the effects of the continued and increasing pressure of population upon the land resources. Competition for jobs is extremely keen and the struggle for mere survival is grim.

In order to pinpoint this colonization, detailed notes were taken on one family that might be considered typical.[8] Tiberio Valderama Gallo is an Antioqueño who, with his wife and family, is working out his salvation as a pioneer in the foothill area south of Sogamoso. As a young man, still a bachelor, he left his native province for the Chocó, where he worked as a mechanic or at any work he could find in connection with a mining enterprise. He saved little money but saw some of the country. In 1935, at age twenty-five, he married María Sánchez, age eighteen, who had had some experience as a nurse. Then for eight years he worked as a carpenter in the province of Antioquia and in the cities of Zipaquirá and Sogamoso. His memories of the back-breaking, soul-depressing labor were still

8. Detailed studies by social anthropologists of social stratification and value systems in the pioneer zone and in the sectors from which the pioneers are coming are yet to be made. It is hoped that this virgin field will soon find workers.

vivid. He longed to get out of this treadmill into something where he would be independent. The opportunity seemed to present itself when a "voluntary" contribution for the marriage of the owner's daughter was requested from the workmen of the small factory in which he was working. He spoke of the poverty of the workmen, of the relative affluence and economic security of the *patrón*, and he rebelled at the thought of having to pinch a contribution out of the bellies of his family, which by then (1942) consisted of five children, in order that the sleek, fat daughter of the owner might have a sumptuous wedding. He departed Sogamoso with his family for the tiny hamlet of Pajarito, which is lost in the midst of the heavily forested, steep mountain slopes. He left his family in a one-room hut and went on without a cent to a plot of ground he was to clear near Cupiagua. For the first two weeks he lived only on cooking bananas, boiled or baked, mixed with salt. He planted small patches of corn, bananas, and yuca. Meanwhile, his wife and children were living on a starvation diet. When a temporary shelter was built on the clearing, she sold her stockings and ironing board to get enough to hire a pack mule on which to load her few belongings. Then she set out on foot for the clearing. The night she arrived they experienced the worst storm of their lives and spent the whole night in fear and trembling. The roof held; it was clear the next day, and both she and her husband said that, in spite of storms, they were glad to be here at the edge of the forest where one was independent. The dominant motive behind the move was the unquenchable desire for independence. He was determined to go forward, to migrate, without looking back. He knew that he had burned his bridges and that it was on the frontier where he must make his living. To be sure, he might send his family away to be educated, but he would carve out of this wilderness the land that would support him and his family. He was here *para siempre* (forever) he said, but he mused awhile before adding, "unless I find another area of colonization in a sector with a somewhat milder climate." He has given some thought to settlement possibilities in that sector of the mountain front between San Martín and Florencia, one of the most attractive areas yet to be settled in the whole country.

His wife María is just as determined to be independent. Fortunately she enjoys good health and can work fourteen to sixteen hours a day. She now has excellent help in her two oldest daughters, who are up early and do a lot of the cooking, but while they were still small their mother did all the household tasks such as cooking, sewing, mending, and bathing of children. Further, she did not hesitate when her husband was away from home or busy at other tasks to do the work herself in the small plots where yuca, plantains, and corn are grown, and to carry the produce home on her back.

By February 1945, everyone was sick with intestinal upsets and malaria, but Tiberio had to go out, alternately shivering with chills and burning with fever, into the dark forest and the rocky grassy hills to hunt for game. It was the only protective food available. The whole family is aware of the importance to health of citrus fruits, and parents and children alike consumed quantities of limes from several old trees near the house that were bearing while the senior author was there. For months it was impossible to get protein, except by hunting. There was no neighbor near enough from whom he might have obtained pork or beef. It was then that he became most keenly aware of the importance of an adequate diet to fortify the human body against the onslaught of disease. Everyone became infected with malaria when the mosquitoes got bad in the dry season, but he was able to send for plasmoquin through a friend and thus cure the sick.

The first year he cleared four acres of land during time off from his job on the road where he earned eighty cents a day. With that money he could buy only the barest essentials in Boquerón. By the end of the second year he had cleared twenty acres of land, had bought a milk cow for twenty-five dollars, and had several pigs and forty chickens. The cow had a calf in two months' time. By 1949 he had built a house and had acquired six cows and eight calves, three hogs, and a sizable flock of chickens. Then came civil war, which rapidly created a social and political climate infinitely more difficult to cope with than the natural environment.

The scourge of the subsistence farmer or the pioneer in so many parts of Latin America has been recurrent revolution or actual civil war. Colombia had been spared this curse for over two generations, but the hatred between conservatives and liberals had merely been smoldering, and in 1948 it burst into flame and destroyed many thriving villages and prosperous farmsteads. Almost the entire valley on the eastern side of the Andes, with Pajarito as its center, was devastated as the bands of conservatives, the government forces, hunted down and destroyed the liberals, giving no quarter. Many people hid out in the forest with little shelter, almost no food, and in constant danger of being ambushed and destroyed. Others returned to the cities, where life was more secure than in the villages or in the open countryside. It became unsafe in this sector even for a conservative Antioqueño because, as the fighting continued and the lust for blood increased in intensity, government forces were apt to shoot first and inquire into political affiliations after.

So Tiberio was forced to sell the land that he had struggled to clear and make productive. He received $1,000 for the cleared land and another $125 for the hogs, chickens, and corn. The fact that, starting with nothing at all, he had been able with five years' hard work to accumulate $1,125 was a great stimulus to him. But unfortunately he was caught again in the same urban treadmill. His earnings as a carpenter were not enough to keep up with inflation, and his savings dwindled rapidly. By the time the civil war had run its course, he was again in desperate financial circumstances, leading a precarious existence in his struggle to support a growing family with wages lagging far behind soaring costs. By 1953 he was anxious either to return to his former holdings or to go somewhere else where settlement was active. His old farm was not for sale, and he had no money with which to buy it. He was glad to enter into an agreement with the owner of 200 acres of land near Cupiagua, whereby he could establish his home, clear land, and harvest crops on the halves.

He came out again in 1953 to build a shelter and plant his food crops—corn, yuca, and plantains. He had a four-year contract with the owner of the land. Everything produced on the farm, not including what was consumed by the family, was on the halves. However, one-third of the value of permanent improvements on the farm, such as coffee bushes and improved pastures, belonged to the renter. Within a year he had cleared twenty acres for pasture and had about five times that amount to clear. It was slow work because he and his brother-in-law, without money to hire men, had to do it alone. Coffee was to be planted later.

He had come out to this land without any knowledge of soils, rainfall conditions, or other physical factors he would have to cope with. He experimented steadily in his kitchen garden to find out what food crops would do best. He grew onions, lettuce, tomatoes, cabbage, squash, carrots, and other vegetables. Cow manure gathered in the nearby, recently cleared pasture was used to fertilize the kitchen garden. Around the house forty mango trees were planted. This is the type of farmer who would and could benefit from technical assistance, preferably on a county agent basis. However, Colombians, like Latin Americans generally, have learned the hard way to distrust those who proffer assistance. Before farmers will be receptive to a technical aid program, even one of, by, and for Colombians, they will have to be convinced that it is really to their interest to cooperate. This has proved to be a formidable task, but progress is being made.

An important factor in the success of the pioneering venture under discussion is family solidarity. Husband and wife and children form a closely knit unit working toward a common goal. Dora and Soe de la Cruz do the house cleaning and cooking. They are up by five o'clock in the morning, to build the fire in the cook shed next to the house and start breakfast. Wood is brought in from the forest by the boys and is cut into usable lengths and split into smaller pieces by Uncle Marco, brother of María, who also helps in clearing the forest. House-cleaning tasks are performed after the men have gone to work and while mother is busy with her sewing. Besides the two daughters mentioned, there are other children: José Ceferino, Omar, Hairo Alonso, Waldemar, Lida de la Cruz, Tiberio Agusto, Gorge Enrique, and José Guillermo. They all have to be regularly bathed, fed, clothed, and "minded," and those jobs take up all the available time of the mother and two oldest daughters. Each child asks and receives his mother's and father's blessing each night, and the family often reads the questions and responses of the *rosario*. Discipline is strict, punishment is swift. Certain precepts are instilled into the children at an early age: parents must be obeyed without question; the older children do not tease the younger ones; food is never to be wasted. When one of the younger children, in a fit of temper, throws his food on the ground, he is soundly spanked.

Further, the Antioqueño—of whom José is one—has the tradition of individual initiative and of economic independence behind him. He has always made his living at a trade or on a little plot of land and has unbounded confidence in himself. He has not, like the Santandereano, been tied to the land in debt bondage till he has lost the capacity to strike out on his own. He still has the will and the optimism to migrate in the hope of finding something better.

PAMPLONA–RÍO FRIO

The population of the little mountain town of Pamplona and its vicinity has in recent years been increasingly subjected to the economic pull of Cúcuta. This pull has counteracted the tendency to migrate southward and eastward toward the llanos of the Arauca River, the boundary between Venezuela and Colombia. The road from Pamplona to Labateca is mainly through the narrow gorge of the Chitagá River, where the growing of crops is difficult; even grazing does not prosper. Labateca and Toledo, established on relatively fertile alluvial terraces, are old settlements, and the cultural landscape between Labateca and Batá is mature—corn, yuca, plantains, beans, and squash are the food crops; coffee and sugarcane are grown for cash. However, as soon as one crosses the high ridge south of Batá on the Margua River, one is in wild, barely settled country. A few men are engaged in burning charcoal and in cutting trees for lumber. The sector is obviously being "mined" of its resources with no plan of permanent settlement. The area should be colonized for strategic reasons, if for no other, and the road should be improved if settlers are to be attracted. An oil strike south of the Arauca River would probably mean that the whole area would, to a large extent, be invaded by Venezuelans looking for work rather than by Colombians.

Pore was reputedly the most important llanos town and, for colonial society, its influence was greater than that of any of the modern capitals. It is said that at one time Pore, extremely rich in cattle, had a larger population than Santa Fé, capital of the viceroyalty.

Guanapalo and Pauto were also thriving economic and cultural centers during colonial times, the epoch of greatest missionary activity. Because of their wealth and the number of their inhabitants, they played an important role in Colombian history. This was a zone of great ranches and thriving towns when the rest of the llanos was still Indian territory.[9]

After the wars of independence, missionary activity declined in the mountain-front sector for a hundred miles or more south of the largely unoccupied Colombia-Venezuela frontier zone; whether it was the cause or the effect of lack of development, it is difficult to determine. At present Colombian nationalism is demanding that

9. Cf. Raye R. Platt.

this unoccupied area between the mountain heartland and the international boundary be filled in. But all growth requires time. Meanwhile, the boundary between Colombia and Venezuela remains to a high degree an artificial line on a map, a broad buffer zone with little significance in reality.

The depression followed in part by the Arauca River, a natural passageway between the Magdalena and Orinoco rivers, was a trade route during the period of La Gran Colombia, when corn from Guasdualito in Apure (Venezuela) was marketed in El Socorro. But this natural trade route was cut when Colombia and Venezuela became separate nations and the Arauca River became the international boundary. The important centers of Venezuela have from the beginning maintained close relations with the llanos, with the result that, since the country achieved independence, the Táchira Depression increased in importance and has continued increasing in importance as Venezuela has tightened its economic grip on the zone bordering Colombia.[10]

Under the republic, however, Colombia neglected its frontier zone, so far away from Bogotá, the center of political power; the mountain centers such as Pamplona did not have the close relations with the llanos that San Cristóbal and Mérida maintained in Venezuela. But in recent years the Colombian government has begun to see the importance of settlements, particularly along the international boundary. A sector along the Sarare River, inhabited by Tunebo Indians and some 80 to 100 miles from Pamplona, has been selected for colonization by INCORA. An office of INCORA was set up at a point to be called Tunebia, between the Cobugón and Covaría rivers, near where they are joined by the Margua River. The project is reached by the road coming from Pamplona, which will be continued on to Tame in the llanos of Casanare.

The zone contains some excellent soils in the 25- to 30-mile-wide strip of the piedmont alluvial plain, in the alluvial terraces and bottom lands (vegas) along the rivers, and in the gallery forests along the rivers out on the llanos. The rainfall is high but fairly well distributed throughout the year, and the vegetation cover consists of tropical rain forests rich in species. It is hoped that settlements in the future will be made along this road, in the transition zone between piedmont forests and open grasslands. Here, climate,

10. Cf. chap. 2, pp. 35–37.

soils, and vegetation are most favorable for human activities. It was precisely here that thriving settlements came into being during the colonial regime and were allowed to decay in the early republican era.

Individual colonists often seem to prefer forested areas; with no capital and little skill, only a tremendous capacity for work, they engage here in slash-and-burn agriculture, clearing and firing the forest and rotating plots instead of crops. This type of agriculture, geared to subsistence crops, differs markedly from that practiced on their tiny plots in the mountains, where they were at least market oriented if they could produce a surplus to sell. Where there is enough good land to attract massive waves of farmers it will be possible for them to create their own autonomous economic centers. The lone peasant with a machete in the forest, producing only for his own needs, will in the years ahead become an anomaly. He does not represent the type of settler who will most effectively tie peripheral regions to the national economy.

Pasto-Mocoa

The road eastward from Pasto, the economic and administrative capital of highland Nariño, can take vehicles up to three tons. The first ten miles, it climbs steeply through an intensively cultivated area of *minifundios* to the pass known as El Tábano (the horse fly), the continental divide, or *divorcio aquarum* (elev.: 10,330 feet); the road descends even more abruptly to the tiny village of El Encano on the shore of the picturesque Laguna de la Cocha—probably of glacial origin.

On a tiny peninsula jutting out into the Laguna is the recently constructed tourist hotel, Sindamanoy, surrounded by a thriving flower garden in a grove of sweet-smelling eucalyptus trees. Here tourists from Pasto, Popayán, or Cáli, or from the hot lowlands of the Putumayo, come to enjoy the delights of trout fishing, motor boating, and hiking in the cold, brisk, rarefied air, or to enjoy the less strenuous pleasure of gazing on the placid waters of the mountain-rimmed Laguna, with its shifting lights and shadows, from the comfortable armchairs of the living room of the hotel. Trails are being extended by small slash-and-burn farmers farther and farther into the virgin lands on both sides of the lake; meat on the hoof, charcoal, potatoes, cabbages, onions, white hand cheese, and so on, are brought to the road for shipment by truck to Pasto or to the hot country of Mocoa and Puerto Asís. Even the local cabinet-maker, an expert craftsman who uses the fine hardwoods of the local forests, has been inundated with orders for modish items of furniture by patrons who live as far away as Bogotá.

Between El Encano and Santiago, another extremely steep mountain must be crossed. On both of its slopes the felling of trees for timber, but particularly for the making of charcoal, is going on at a dizzy pace, with little thought of control measures to safeguard soil and water resources. Between Santiago and San Francisco, via the village of Sibundoy, seat of the Capuchin Mission, the road hugs the base of the steep north slope of a vast swampy basin, now drained by the Putumayo River, that must originally have been overdeepened by glacial action. Settlers have cleared the forest from the well-drained and fertile alluvial fans deposited by the streams that empty into the swamp and have established thriving cattle ranches.

The San Francisco–Mocoa sector crosses still another high pass, the Páramo of Bichoy, before plunging eastward through many miles of wild, rocky country, completely inhospitable to human settlement. From the last defile, at about 6,500 feet, one can discern in clear weather the great valleys of the Putumayo and Caquetá rivers with the tiny settlements along them. From there the road descends 3,200 feet in 15 miles to Pepino, 6 miles from Mocoa, long the capital of the Comisaría of Putumayo; it has three long streets cut by six short ones, wide and well marked. The authorities work and live in relatively commodious municipal buildings.

Puerto Limón, Urcusique, and Puerto Umbría are all tiny bridgeheads in the wilderness settled mostly by hard-working people from Nariño, Antioquia, and Caldas.

The Comisaría of Putumayo is the home of three cultural, racial, and linguistic groups of Indians—the Ingano, Siona, and Kofán—who were originally well adjusted to their environment but whose economy and social organization were primitive. The settlers from the mountains exploited these Indians and took advantage of them in many ways, with the result that the Indians have fled to areas yet untouched by the new settlers. The cultural inferiority of those few who remain, to be seen in the Sibundoy Valley and around Mocoa, is reflected in their low social and economic standing in the community where they are a prey to malaria, yellow fever, influenza, and water-borne diseases as well as to their "civilized" fellowman. These primitive people are given little help toward improving their agricultural techniques, although even now they supply many of the "spearheads of penetration" with yuca, plantain, corn, and vegetables. Nor is their artistry—pottery, baskets, and textiles—valued very highly by the local elite. Yet some of the finer examples are veritable museum pieces.[11]

Some of the settlers who came as the Pasto-Mocoa road was opened had a little capital and a small fund of experience in living and in making a living in frontier zones; the great majority were men whose only baggage consisted of their capacity for hard work. The settlers were a heterogeneous lot—poverty-stricken day laborers, sharecroppers, or renters from the large estates in the hot lowlands or temperate highlands; half-starved peasant proprietors of tiny, fragmented plots in the cold country. Here was a vast fertile country awaiting settlement where land could be had for the taking. All a settler had to do was to build a thatch hut, clear a piece of forest with his machete, and plant corn, yuca, and plantains. But this was not enough to cope with the new environment. Weakened by a poor diet, a settler was ready prey to malaria and other diseases that still further undermined him. With no capital it was impossible to buy drugs, even if they had been available. Many of the early settlers died; in many settlements *all* the children died year after year. Once sick and ailing, a worker is no longer able to keep up the unequal struggle against the forest; there would be much less sickness if public health measures were systematically undertaken to kill the vectors of tropical fevers and to decrease the incidence of waterborne diseases. Further, cheap and easy credit should be available to the settler without his having to go through endless red tape; thus he could bring his agricultural equipment and techniques up to date and take care of his seasonal needs without recourse to the usurer. Finally, improved roads would tie the settler more securely to his local market and thereby to the national economy.

The mountainous area around Ipiales, near the border with Ecuador, is also seeking a safety valve to the east in the form of one road via La Victoria to connect with the San Miguel River, and another via Puerres, which crosses a pass in the cordillera and will connect with the Guamués River which drains the Laguna de la Cocha.

11. Milcíades Chaves Ch., "La colonización de la Comisaría del Putumayo: un problema etno-económico-geográfico de importancia nacional."

The state of Cauca has completed the road from El Bordo to Bolívar and every effort should be made to continue this on to San Sebastián and thence, crossing the divide, to Santa Rosa on the Caquetá. Santa Rosa should then be tied to Mocoa and Puerto Limón. This accomplished, the road following the foot of the cordillera from Florencia to Puerto Limón, via Belén, would open up a vast fertile area to settlement.

The Upper Putumayo watershed has a population of 60,000, of whom 90 per cent live within one-half mile of the road, the river and its navigable tributaries, the four roadspurs, or the six major trails. The areas of origin of recent settlers there coincide neatly with those areas of extremely inequitable land tenure and of marked rural discontent. A few energetic individuals, victims of rural poverty, are sometimes able to break with the tradition of poverty by emigrating. If they report favorably on their new home, relatives or former neighbors will follow. Every second immigrant (of the 900 heads of families interviewed) had as his motivation for immigrating the acquisition of land as his final goal. By far the greater number of migrants had moved of their own initiative, neither expecting nor receiving public aid. Ninety per cent of the immigrants came to the Putumayo directly from their place of birth, showing that they knew what they wanted and had the will to obtain it against all odds. Living levels are definitely higher than they were before migration, as a strong class of farmers with medium-sized properties has emerged. Problems of primitive living conditions, of tropical soil management, of climate and health, are not looked upon by the settlers as major impediments to development.

In his dissertation on the Upper Putumayo Basin, Rolf Wesche[12] concludes that the highest priority desiderata necessary to achieve overall regional development are: the continued construction of roads, plus government provision of rural educational facilities and public health measures; short-term credit and property titling services; the introduction of regular service with shallow-draft, diesel-powered barges or tugs on the Putumayo River below Puerto Asís to eliminate the excessively high charges of middlemen; and a restriction of property frontage per owner on all transportation arteries in order to insure more rapid spatial spread in, and consequent intensive development of, the hinterland.

12. "The Settler Wedge of the Upper Putumayo River" (Ph.D. diss., University of Florida, 1967).

Oil.—Oil was first discovered in the Orito field in southwestern Colombia in 1963, and within three years fifteen producing wells had been completed with a production of some 30,000 to 40,000 barrels a day. An early 1969 target date was met for moving this oil to market by pipeline. The 193-mile-long Trans-Andean pipeline scales the Andes at an 11,500-foot pass before descending to Tumaco on the Pacific coast. Designed for an initial through-put capacity of 50,000 barrels a day, this can be increased to 150,000 barrels a day by the addition of more pumps. This increase in capacity may be necessary when production mounts in two other fields in the general area which were discovered in 1965. Gulf and Texaco have concessions of more than 3 million acres in southern Colombia and additional concessions across the border in Ecuador. Operations on this large scale will continue to be a magnet for immigrants who will do a thriving business producing food for a ready market.

This is certainly a major oilfield (one estimated to contain at least 100 million barrels), for oil companies would not have invested some $130 million in exploration, drilling, production facilities, and pipeline construction unless they were certain of substantial reserves.

The pumping station is at Orito, connected by road to Puerto Asís, along which new thatched huts are being built by newcomers to the area, mostly from the Andes. Clearings were made on which to grow more cash crops or to plant pastures for the cattle that were rapidly brought in. By 1966 cattle were grazing in lush pastures that only a few years before had been dense forest. Large dugout canoes powered by outboard motors are the main form of transport along the Putumayo River and supply the brisk riverbank market with sacks of rice and corn, stems of cooking bananas, chickens, pigs, and animal hides. The building of the pipeline to Tumaco necessitated the improvement of the Puerto Asís narrow gravel road, although a great deal of the equipment was brought in by helicopter. First refining of Orito crude is in an onsite refinery with a 1,000 b/d capacity to supply fuel for the local demand.

Reconnaissance mapping of millions of acres in the Llanos Orientales (Eastern Plains) and test drilling of likely structures will be carried out by Ecopetrol (the government oil company), as well as by foreign companies, over the next few years. Such activities will stimulate economic development in many sectors and will be a great stimulus to immigrants interested in agriculture.

OVERVIEW

Four decades ago F. O. Martin felt that the three chief drawbacks to settlement and development of the llanos-Andes border area of Colombia were the lack of kept-up roads and trails, a good labor force, and community spirit. He felt keenly about the latter, complaining that "there is no community spirit among the inhabitants in the matter of maintaining trails or in any other communal relations. Cooperation is unknown; rather, intense jealousy among individuals prevails."[13] It has been seen that, although in Colombia as elsewhere miracles are rare in the affairs of men, improvement has been steady: roads and trails are being kept up and improved, and the labor force is not only more numerous than when Martin wrote, but it is more efficient because of a better diet and a lower incidence of the so-called tropical diseases. The community spirit cannot be said to have become Utopian, but it has certainly changed for the better generally, in spite of the temporary setback resulting from the revolutionary outburst of 1950–53. Of fewer and fewer sectors can it be said "settled but unexplored," for the reality is that population pressure in the mountain areas has built up to such an extent that a wave of migrants is actually crossing the eastern cordillera at many points to enter the tropical lowland. The physical climate is one that can more readily be coped with if collective man surrounds himself with a favorable political, social, and economic climate.

As Marston Bates says, tropical forests are not unfriendly; they are merely disinterested. It is understandable why they do *seem* unfriendly when they are attacked by a lone individual, armed only with a machete, who, besides being poorly fed and poorly housed, may be suffering from fever and intestinal ailments and parasites. The picture changes completely when man is in cultural control and can create his own favorable habitat as he penetrates the forest or any other natural landscape he has decided to live in or change. A young officer in Florencia pointed out that any place can be a pesthole if one eats poorly and takes none of the ordinary precautions to maintain health. He concluded that, by merely minimizing and guarding against the bad features of the tropical climate and taking advantage of the good ones, one could lead a very pleasant life there. And thousands of his compatriots are finding this to be

13. "Explorations in Colombia," p. 628.

true, no longer regarding the forces of nature as terrors to be placated, but rather as beneficent powers with which man may cooperate.

There has been no steady pushing back of the frontier on a broad front; rather the forest has been encroached upon in widely scattered areas for the exploitation of whatever resource has been most highly prized at the time. For centuries, minerals or forest products, such as rubber and quinine, played that role. As the mountain population slowly began to recognize the soil of the rain forest as an important, valuable, exploitable resource, they were able to effect what might be termed a breakthrough into the Andean foothills and tropical lowlands in the Villavicencio and Florencia sectors where they are now rapidly consolidating their gains. The temporary breakthrough south from Sogamoso has been largely halted by an unfavorable political climate, while Pamplona is not yet successfully tied to the plains area to the south. Settlers from the mountain sectors of southwest Colombia are in the process of effecting their breakthrough to the east, along the highways mentioned, but thus far various factors have made it impossible for them to anchor themselves by permanent agriculture and grazing. New roads are being constructed only very slowly, and roads already open have not been too well maintained; education and public health campaigns have been neglected; the capacities of the indigenous Indian population have not been fully realized.

The tragedy of the llanos is the tragedy of a frontier zone that, by its very nature, is not yet able to live a life of its own—somewhat like our own Middle West a century ago. As long as the Middle West led a kind of colonial existence vis-à-vis the eastern seaboard it could not work out its own regional salvation. Once it was settled by an industrious, agricultural people and was crisscrossed with railroads and motor roads for intraregional as well as interregional trade, it could and did develop its own complementary industrial society. With the introduction of adequate roads and transportation facilities, education and public health measures, and permanent rather than nomadic agriculture by a vigorous and hard-working people, the llanos may indeed experience an evolution similar in many respects to that of our Middle West during the first half of the nineteenth century.

The densely populated Andean heartland of the nation is being subjected to centrifugal forces that are already undermining its immemorial dominance. Although the center of gravity is still in the cool to cold mountain sectors, the frontier of settlement is actually on the march into the low-lying hot country.

Access roads from the Andes to lowlands in Venezuela and Colombia (Mérida to Barinas and San Cristóbal to Guasdualito in Venezuela; Bogotá to Villavicencio and Neiva to Florencia in Colombia) would seem to show that such roads do indeed support rational economic and demographic development. Many roads have been built almost at random with no advance studies of any kind and with insufficient funds, at the whims of local bigwigs, national politicians, and land speculators. More and more it will prove to be most advantageous for all concerned for roads to be built within the framework of a national plan drawn up with long-range but attainable goals. Those interested in sponsoring settlement should learn that the pioneer cannot be expected indefinitely to accept infinitesimally low prices for his produce induced by monopolistic truck rates; nor will he be content in his new and unfamiliar home if he escapes the serf-like patrón relationship only to become permanently indebted to an Agrarian Reform Agency for modern conveniences that he would rather do without.

A perceptive observer who has carried out careful and extensive field investigations in the frontier zone of eastern Colombia has just published a most informative volume in which he concludes:

The Llanos are not prairies which yield abundantly and consistently by their natural fertility, and the tropical forests are not like the benign temperate woodlands which allow clearing with relative ease and even provide a harvest of timber in the process. The climate in interior tropical South America is not of the seasonally favorable type, but afflicted with the pernicious and continuous extremes of heat and moisture.

And the contrast with the North American frontier is undoubtedly more pronounced in the human sphere. The few hundred thousands which have crossed the Andes in Colombia are not the avant-garde of millions of people who would follow in the path of the frontiersman, settle in the immediate hinterland, "consolidate" it, and provide a ready market and supply zone for the pioneers. The trans-Andean frontier remains physically separated from the core areas of the country whose development is not dependent on progress in the Llanos. Colombia does not move eastward behind her eastern frontier. But the time has come for the nation to realize that it can no longer afford to leave the Eastern Plains in a state of semi-abandonment.[14]

14. Dieter Brunnschweiler, *The Llanos Frontier of Colombia*, Latin American Studies Center, Monograph no. 9 (Michigan State University, 1972), p. 62.

REFERENCES: COLOMBIA

Bates, Marston. "Climate and Vegetation in the Villavicencio Region of Eastern Colombia." *Geographical Review* 38, no. 4 (October 1948):555–74.

Bingham, Hiram. *The Journal of an Expedition across Venezuela and Colombia, 1906–1907*. New Haven: Yale Publishing Association, 1909.

Brücher, Wolfgang. *Die Erschliessung des tropischen Regenwaldes am Ostrand der Kolumbianischen Anden: Der Raum zwischen Rio Ariari und Ecuador.* Tübingen: Geographisches Institut der Universität Tübingen, 1968.

———. "Posibilidades económicas en la región amazónica de Colombia." *Revista de la Cámara de Comercio Colombo-Alemana*, no. 33 (Abril–Junio 1967), pp. 29–36.

Brunnschweiler, Dieter. *The Llanos Frontier of Colombia*. Latin American Studies Center, Monograph no. 9 (Michigan State University, 1972).

Chaves Ch., Milcíades. "La colonización de la Comisaría del Putumayo: un problema etno-económico-geográfico de importancia nacional." *Boletín de Arqueología* 1, no. 6 (Noviembre-Diciembre, 1945):567–98.

Crist, Raymond E., and Guhl, Ernesto. "Pioneer Settlement in Eastern Colombia." *Smithsonian Institution Report for 1956*. Washington, 1957.

Duff, Ernest A. "Agrarian Reform in Colombia: Colonization or Parcelization." *Inter-American Economic Affairs* 18, no. 3 (Winter 1964):39–51.

Eidt, Robert C. "Modern Colonization as a Facet of Land Development in Colombia, South America." *Yearbook of the Association of Pacific Coast Geographers* 29 (1967):21–42.

———. "Pioneer Settlement in Colombia." *Geographical Review* 58, no. 2 (April 1968):298–300.

Guhl, Ernesto. "La colonización del Sarare carece de dirección científica." *Cromos* 89, no. 2230 (March 21, 1960):30–35.

———. "Se adelanta como es debido la colonización campesina en Colombia?" *Cromos* 89, no. 2229 (March 14, 1960):29–33.

Havens, A. Eugene, and Flinn, William L., eds. *Internal Colonialism and Structural Change in Colombia*. Praeger Special Studies in International Economics and Development. New York: Frederick A. Praeger, 1970.

Martin, F. O. "Explorations in Colombia." *Geographical Review* 19, no. 4 (October 1929):621–37.

Pérez, Felipe. *Jeografía física i política de los Estados Unidos de Colombia.* Bogotá: Imprenta de la Nación, 1862.

Reichel-Dolmatoff, G. *Colombia*. Ancient Peoples and Places Series, vol. 44. New York: Frederick A. Praeger, 1965.

Rice, Hamilton. "Further Explorations in the Northwest Amazon Basin." *Geographical Journal* 44, no. 2 (August 1914):137–68.

Stoddart, D. R., and Trubshaw, J. D. "Colonization in Action in Eastern Colombia." *Geography* 47 (January 1962):47–53.

Tinnermeier, Ronald L. *New Land Settlement in the Eastern Lowlands of Colombia*. Research Paper of the Land Tenure Center, no. 13. Madison: University of Wisconsin, 1964.

Wesche, Rolf Jürgen. "The Settler Wedge of the Upper Putumayo River." Ph.D. dissertation, University of Florida, 1967.

4. Ecuador

Ecuador is divided physically in its climate, landscape, and culture. The massive, cool-to-cold Andean cordilleras strewn with volcanoes, most of which are extinct, and the intermontane valleys contain all the important towns, except Guayaquil, and 51 per cent of the country's people. The great majority of the inhabitants are Indians who cling to their cloistered way of life; they have little national feeling and are generally uninterested in large-scale commerce. West of the Andes, the hot, generally low and damp coastal plain is peopled by Indians, Negroes, and mestizos who grow most of the country's export crops and carry on most of its commerce. East of the Andes, the great, hot, forested plain of the Oriente, through which meander the headwater tributaries of the Amazon, is nearly empty, with only 2 per cent of Ecuador's population. Currently it is of almost no economic significance in the agricultural sector.

The forests of Ecuador's "Wild East" begin at the tree line on the eastern flank of the eastern cordillera, cover the mountains and hill lands of the mountain front, and extend in unbroken treescape eastward to the Putumayo River and to the disputed border with Peru. In spite of—perhaps because of—the activities in this vast area of sixteenth-century gold miners and more recent rubber gatherers and adventurers, permanent settlements have been established only with the greatest difficulty. The Jesuit missions of the seventeenth century did not have church leadership long enough to put an indelible stamp on the country as did the Jesuit "reductions" along the Río de la Plata. Building a road into a sparsely settled area such as the Ecuadorian Oriente does not always attract immigrants.

It should always be kept in mind that a highway is built and used for two-way traffic. If a road is built from a densely populated sector X, to a frontier zone, Y, in which a sparse population is precariously

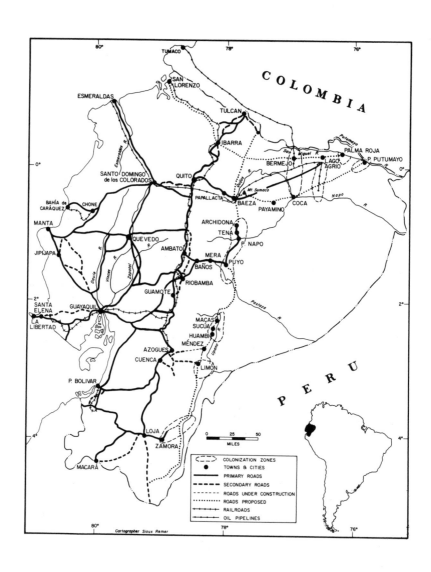

established, the road can be a boon to the people of Y, for they can now send produce to and import goods from X. However, if an epidemic should break out, or if the political situation should become menacing, or if other physical or man-made catastrophes should arise, then the role of the road is reversed. That is, people will use it to flee from X in order to achieve the relative safety of Y, and X will be drained of its inhabitants. A case in point is the Oriente of Ecuador, where the Jesuits established more or less prosperous missions among the Indians in the seventeenth century. When the Jesuits were expelled by the Spanish crown in the eighteenth century, their charges became a prey to rapacious ranchers, miners, and traders looking for cheap or free labor.

PALMA ROJA

A military colonization project in the Amazon Basin, Palma Roja, began in 1962 on the right bank of the San Miguel River in the northeast Ecuadorian Oriente. Funded by the Alliance for Progress, the project is the cooperative effort of the Ministry of Defense, Acción Cívica, and a two-man military mission from the United States.

Rolf Wesche provided the following description of the colony:

... the project still has the appearance of a construction camp when visited. ... One complex of 10 cement-block settler homes has been completed. Four of these are occupied by administrative personnel, and already are scarred with signs of dilapidation. On the opposite end of the bluff on which the village is being built, an identical complex is under construction. The center of the settlement is composed of several workshops, a 6.7-kilowatt diesel-power plant, a barracks for the army construction workers, and a two-room school. Further plans include a church, central store, civic center, and a cemetery. Land has already been cleared for an 800-meter air strip and a soccer field. Slippery clay roads connect the various parts of the settlement. Considering the duration of construction activity, the involvement of an entire company of soldiers (about 60 men), 20 veteran settlers, 2 trucks and 2 tractors, and the interest of the government in the venture's success, the rate of progress seems disappointing.

As happens so often in Latin America, the plans for an orderly settlement have already been diluted. Huts of non-military settlers are sprouting in and around the village. Veterans, unable to wait for the completion of their homes in the village, have built houses on the plots assigned to them along the river.[1]

The twenty veterans, all with a minimum of fifteen years in the military and thus familiar with life in the Oriente, form the nucleus of this service and regional development center; their plots, fronting 220 yards along the river, may not be sold during the first ten years of occupancy. New nonmilitary settlers and increased applications from the military auger well for continued growth.

But Palma Roja, its construction motivated also by Ecuador's need to secure the border zone, yet without a tie-in to the nation's road network, cannot survive without trading across the nearby Colombian-Ecuadorian frontier. Although insisting on supplying the settlement strictly from Ecuadorian sources during its embryonic state, the Ecuadorian government has not followed this policy of certain isolation but has permitted across-the-border movement. The colony, with a population of 250, sees for itself an increasing role in the Oriente's development.

PETROLEUM

It was generally assumed that the accord signed in 1942 in Rio de Janeiro had settled a long-standing boundary dispute between Ecuador and Peru. However, as far as Ecuador is concerned, there is still a zone in dispute (zona controvertida) in the southern part of the country. Vast quantities of petroleum have been discovered in southwestern Colombia, in the northeastern Oriente of Ecuador, and more recently (1972) in the Pavayacú area, some 150 miles west of Iquitos, in northwestern Peru. This is a powerful motivation behind the determination of the Ecuadorian government to incorporate the Oriente into the national economy. With the rapid development of large oil fields nearby in the Putumayo basin of Colombia, active oil exploration in Ecuador's Oriente has suddenly rejuvenated the area, now patterned with large concessions. In April 1967, Texas Gulf Oil Company spudded in its first wildcat at Lago Agrio, forty-five miles southeast of Colombia's Orito field. In May, thirty miles west at Bermejo, the company struck oil in a second wildcat and in August completed a second producing well at Lago

1. Rolf Jürgen Wesche, "The Settler Wedge of the Upper Putumayo River," pp. 267–68.

Agrio. To the south, at Coca on the Napo River, the company has spudded in a fourth well. On concessions of nine other companies, aeromagnetic surveys are being carried out as well as photogeological studies; other companies are engaged in seismograph surveys.

Ecuador, with reserves estimated at 5 to 7 billion barrels, may soon become South America's largest oil exporter. The Ecuadorian State Petroleum Corporation (CEPE) was established in 1972 to coordinate this new industry.

Millions of dollars are being invested in the Oriente in connection with the further development of oil fields; thousands of floating laborers have been attracted to this area, but very few of them come with the goal of becoming permanent residents engaged in agricultural pursuits. Indeed, some who have been producing crops on small plots abandon them to seek employment at high wages in the oil field. However, once production is stabilized, it is estimated that the services of a total of not more than 500 to 1,000 full-time employees will be required to operate the oil field, service the recently completed (July 1972) pipeline from the oil-producing area to Esmeraldas, and care for the storage tanks and port installations in Esmeraldas. When this time arrives, there will be unemployment, outmigration, and economic depression in the area, as has been the case with the Orito oil field across the border in Colombia.

Such conditions do not favor effective settlement of rain forest lands, as many of those who come to make their fortune in the oil fields have neither the spirit of the pioneer nor a penchant for the sedentary life of the farmer. Perhaps the government is anticipating this eventuality, for one reads in the *Alliance for Progress Weekly Newsletter* (September 18, 1972) that a mixed highway-waterway known as the "Inter-Oceanic Way" is being built to connect the Ecuadorian seaport of San Lorenzo to the river port of Manaus, State of Amazonas, Brazil. A highway will link San Lorenzo to Puerto Putumayo on the Putumayo River; the remaining distance to Manaus is to be covered by riverboats.

PENETRATION ROADS TO THE EAST

The road eastward from Quito crosses two deep gorges in semi-arid country and ascends to a very high, cold pass before the descent to Papallacta. In 1970 this road was improved by the oil company and extended to the producing field at Lago Agrio, via Baeza.

Most of the easily accessible land along the Quito–Lago Agrio road was rapidly occupied by spontaneous colonists. A town, Nueva Loja, grew up near the Texaco-Gulf Camp, consisting originally of a muddy street, without sidewalks, lined with primitive bars and ramshackled restaurants and rooming houses. The population of Nueva Loja in early 1973 numbered about 2,000; small but substantial stores handling general merchandise and notions were being built, and property lines were being laid out according to the specifications of the Instituto Ecuatoriano de Reforma Agraria y Colonización (IERAC).

Some 10,000 settlers, largely from the drought-stricken Loja Province and the northern coastal provinces, have come into the whole Aguarico region. Those living outside the town are for the most part engaged in subsistence farming pro tem, that is, their immediate goal is to raise as much of their own food as possible, but they hope in the future to produce some surplus for the Sierran market with which to buy such staples as sugar, rice, and potatoes, and clothing, tools, and household utensils. Hence, they settled on or as near as possible to the roads that give them access to the markets of the Sierra.

The road from Ambato eastward has long been open as far as Baños. Even before there was a road for wheeled vehicles, people came on horseback to bathe in the hot mineral springs there. In the 1930s the Shell Oil Company opened the road as far as Mera, drilled a few dry holes, and abandoned the well sites. The few floaters who came in at that time as laborers drifted away. During the earthquake of 1949, the town of Pelileo, between Ambato and Baños, was deeply buried under a tremendous landslide of millions of tons of volcanic ash. This horrible catastrophe cast its shadow on road construction for several years. Even twenty years after the event the new town called Pelileo, built on a steep barren slope not far from its buried predecessor, was far from flourishing. In spite of frequent landslides and washouts, the road is kept open and has been continued as far as Tena on the Napo River. A small but steady trickle of settlers is coming in and the faithful *mistos* (trucks that haul both freight and passengers) have regularly scheduled service from Baños to Tena and from Baños to Quito.

UPANO RIVER VALLEY

Between the forested Cordillera Oriental and the Cordillera Cucutá, extending approximately from Méndez northward to Macas at an altitude of 1,700–3,700 feet, there is one area of the Ecuadorian Oriente priming for incorporation into the national economy: the relatively flat Upano River Valley, an area recently designated by the Junta de Planificacíon as one of the most important for colonization. Previously, some adjacent highland settlers, two or three thousand from Cuenca, imbued with a desire for adventure or merely tired of trying to live on the pittance to be earned making Panamá, or *jipijapa*, hats, came to the Upano River Valley to search for gold near Méndez. Here, despite very hard work, they seldom make more than a bare living, but they are noticeably better off than they were in the uplands. And from these uplands additional waves of migrants have poured into highland cities and the Southeast Oriente, fleeing periodic droughts, heavy erosion on the agricultural lands, and extreme *minifundia*.

There are already 15,000 squatters in the valley, utilizing 100,000 acres of land primarily for the raising of cattle. Scattered along the left side of the Upano are Jíbaro Indians who, because of mission encouragement and training, have shown a tendency to trade their nomadic way of life for one more permanent. The completion of the primary penetration roads to Méndez and beyond will permit the immediate settlement of 1,150 families; another 3,100 families will be settled later on 280,000 acres, approximately 75 acres planned per family. But now these are only paper exercises. The plans, yet to be fully implemented, call for the selection of *colonos* and aid for their migration (only those with private resources are now entering the zone of colonization, excluding those who are barely subsisting on small, drought- and erosion-plagued sierra plots). There will also be secondary roads, construction of schools, medical dispensaries, a cold storage warehouse for meat, experimental farms, marketing and consumer cooperatives, titling of properties by the IERAC,[2] all to be financed by a $3 million loan from the Interamerican Development Bank for road construction and $6 million from national agencies for colonization costs.

With the bank loan, construction of the roads to and within this frontier zone is progressing. A major penetration route to Méndez, considered in 1949 and finally decided upon in 1962, has reached

2. From 1964 to September 30, 1967, 728 families received title to 50,000 acres of land. An additional 190,000 acres are now being titled (Instituto Ecuatoriano de Reforma Agraria y Colonización, *Estadísticas de las realizaciones en reforma agraria y colonización* [Quito, 1968]) .

the Negro River, eighty miles from Cuenca. A road within the valley extending south from Macas, as of mid-1968, was inching south, six miles east of Méndez, eventually to be joined with the penetration road and with a proposed intravalley road from Limón. Limón is the terminus of a completed second penetration road from Cuenca. Seventy miles of short secondary roads, eight miles of which are completed, will cut from both sides of the Upano River, east and west into more virgin territory. When completed, this road network will funnel the products of the region's major economic activity, cattle raising, to the Sierra. Cattle are now removed by airplane. An estimated 50 per cent of crop production in the valley now rots because of the lack of inexpensive means of reaching highland markets. With roads, trucks will haul out coffee, yuca, rice, peanuts, plantains, citrus, soybeans, nuts from the wild almond tree, and so on. Now almost all crops are grown for subsistence by primitive agricultural methods, by colonos waiting for the colonization project to move beyond government offices.

A case study: Macas and Sucuá.—The towns of Macas and Sucuá are located in the zone of active colonization in the Upano River Valley; both have been described by Richard Hansis.[3] His findings are included here to compare and contrast two Oriente frontier towns, one geared to the traditional, the other to the innovative.

The contrast between Macas, a settlement for over 360 years, and Sucuá, a relatively new town of approximately 40 years, is striking. The inhabitants of Macas are, for the most part, descendants of *serranos* who came several centuries ago from the Sierra and have historical ties with Guamote and Riobamba. Cuenca, as the early center for expeditions to this part of the Oriente, lost its influence after the founding of Riobamba. The trail leading to Cuenca served Macas as a connection to other settlements in the valley and occasionally as a means to market products. Macas is dominated by the inertia of centuries. Several families are important because of early connections. Sucuá, however, has not had to break with heavy traditions and has not been saddled with similar problems. Sucuá is freer to choose a more pragmatic approach towards solving problems and encouraging growth.

Length of settlement plays a part in the distribution of houses within the two towns. The central plazas of both Macas and Sucuá are roughly comparable, but the scattered location of buildings

3. "Colonization in the Upano River Valley, Ecuador."

around the plaza in Macas contrasts with the compactness of buildings around the plaza in Sucuá, and this pattern holds throughout the towns. In Macas, the early pattern of scattered homestead sites surrounded by subsistence crops, fruit trees, sugarcane, and pasture continues. Sucuá, although the homesites are somewhat spaced out, has a more compact settlement form and has several streets near the central plaza with wall-to-wall houses.

Macas does not accept newcomers and especially does not like colonos from Cuenca, for the long-time residents fear erosion of their positions of economic and social superiority. They see Cuencanos as special villains because these people seem to have a knack for business. The Spanish background of many of the residents is also a possible reason for the coldness toward Indian and mestizo migrants from the Sierra provinces. The population of Macas in 1858 was around 370; in 1912, 490; by 1960, 1,800; in 1968, an estimated 2,000. Families are exceptionally large, thus providing a pool of cheap labor. Inbreeding is prevalent; consequent physical and mental defects such as albinism and mental retardation seem especially common.

Sucuá does not have the closed atmosphere found in Macas. Its inhabitants accept newcomers, since they themselves are relatively recent colonos. The jealousy of Cuenca is not found here, in fact many of the migrants are from the province of Azuay (capital, Cuenca). The doubling of the population of the urban area of Sucuá in three years (1965–68) has resulted in a population of about 2,300. Growth is mainly the result of migration.

The tradition-bound people of Macas seem unable to unite in group effort. Petty quarrels inhibit the effective functioning of groups such as men's and women's Red Cross clubs. Most of the leadership is provided by the Salesian Mission, several foreign immigrants, and Peace Corps volunteers. Sucuá, on the other hand, does not have these problems. Here, dynamic individuals have led in the organization of several groups that have proved effective. A radio station in Sucuá is the result of individual effort and entrepreneurship; Macas does not have one. The movie theater in Macas was built by the Salesian Mission several years ago, while the one-year-old theater in Sucuá is the result of private initiative.

Macas has a credit cooperative founded in 1965 with 35 members and a capitalization of $580. By the end of 1967, it had grown to 99 members and $4,200. The credit cooperative in Sucuá has more members and greater capitalization. Financial support and advice from both national and international cooperative organizations are available. The members were able to obtain this aid through planning and perseverance, qualities which also are found in Macas but are limited by the lack of internal harmony and dynamic leadership.

Macas, as capital of the province of Morona-Santiago, has government offices and agencies not found in Sucuá. The only existing agricultural extension agency, manned by a veterinarian and an extension agent, is found in Macas; there are plans for one in Sucuá. Macas also has a national health agency and a new clinic which are not found in Sucuá. On closer inspection, this does not amount to much in differential development of the towns, for Sucuá does have a hospital in the mission where most people go with serious health problems.

Sucuá's equal to the extension agency in Macas is the office of the Instituto Nacional de Reforma Agraria y Colonización which operates five days a week to demarcate lands and help colonos secure clear titles. The office opens only on Friday and Saturday mornings in Macas. This operation is a result of the colonization activity taking place in the areas surrounding the two settlements. In 1964, the *parroquia* (parish) of Sucuá showed 6 families receiving 1,140 acres; in 1965, 186 families received 6,485 acres; in 1966, 63 families received title to 4,020 acres; until September 30, no land had been titled in 1967. The only year that the parroquia of Macas showed titling activity was in 1966, when 12 acres were petitioned for and granted.

Another factor that sets Sucuá apart from Macas is its multipurpose center presently under construction. Since Sucuá lies about halfway between Macas and Méndez, and is near the site where a bridge will be built across the Upano River, it will be the center of convergence for the entire valley. In addition to its probable position as the center of commercial activity, it will also become an administrative center in spite of the fact that Macas is the provincial capital. The multipurpose center will be the general administrative seat for Centro de Reconversión Económica del Azuay, Cañar, y Morona-Santiago (CREA) and Instituto Ecuatoriano de Reforma Agraria y Colonización officials in the Upano Valley. Sucuá will also have a refrigerated warehouse for meat storage, eliminating the last-minute slaughtering of cattle only when airplanes can land.

Both Macas and Sucuá have agencies of the Banco Nacional de Fomento. However, the one in Sucuá has a greater amount of money loaned. The rationale behind this difference lies in the colonos' outlook and socioeconomic position. The recent colonos of Sucuá are more receptive to change and new ideas than the large native-born population of Macas. The colonos of Sucuá need money and are ready to obtain it. The colono in Macas is possibly more economically secure—he usually has, at the minimum, ten head of cattle— than his counterpart in Sucuá and is less open to new ideas. His propensity for obtaining a loan is much lower than that of the colono of Sucuá.

The Salesian Mission in Macas is strong; its pervasive activities may be one of the reasons for lack of innovation. Although this arm of the Roman Catholic Church has brought education, the first electric lights in the Upano Valley, and the only movie theater in Macas, little change can take place without its approval. For example, a girl in the area's only *colegio*, run by the mission, worked in political support of the Socialist party and was suspended from school; the girls working for the Conservative party were not. A Peace Corps volunteer was also removed from her teaching position in the mission school for encouraging women's groups. The strength of the Salesian Mission is less in Sucuá. This is surprising, given the fact that the migrants come from poor parts of the Sierra which is heavily dominated by the church. One possible explanation for its lessened influence is the existence of a strong Protestant Mission directed by a dynamic and enterprising missionary, who was instrumental in the building of the first airstrip in the Upano Valley and brought the first plane to Sucuá in 1946. His work for over twenty-five years has been of incalculable value for Sucuá. The Protestant influence is negligible in Macas, for the Salesian Mission's strength has hampered the work of the Protestants.

Since the schools are almost entirely mission-run, they reflect some of the differences between the missions of the two settlements. Macas with its colegio has an advantage over Sucuá in secondary education. However, Sucuá has the advantage of trade and agricultural instruction that should prove to be more practical for the colonos.

Other facilities are distributed more or less equally between the two communities. Both have airstrips, although Sucuá has more flights due to the greater amount of meat leaving. On a weekly basis, Sucuá ships out 30,000 to 32,000 pounds of meat to market in the

Sierra and beyond; Macas sends only 12,000 to 15,000 pounds. Meat from Sucuá, sent immediately upon slaughter at the airport and without any protection, is loaded on DC-3's and flown to Cuenca. From Cuenca, it may go as far as Guayaquil or northern Peru. Meat butchered in Macas is wrapped in cheesecloth-type covering and taken from the slaughterhouse by truck. Four meat-transport flights per week carry the beef to Pastaza, in the Oriente to the north, where it is loaded on trucks and hauled to Sierra communities.

The recent extension of the road south of Huambi and Logroño has greatly facilitated the transportation of beef from Sucuá. Slightly higher prices in Sucuá may explain why cattle are trucked or driven by night from the Macas zone to Sucuá to be slaughtered. This movement from canton to canton is illegal. There is also draining of cattle in the Sucuá zone without regard for the future. Strong efforts should be made to encourage building up of herds before the penetration road is completed. The zone of commerce of Macas is not as large as that of Sucuá because of the limits imposed by the lack of roads and trails and the consequent lack of colonos to the north.

Physical geography accounts for only a small part of the variation. Although there is a difference in altitude between Macas (3,000 feet) and Sucuá (2,400 feet), this is not too important. It is true that the slightly warmer temperatures may have a minimal effect on the rate of growth and types of crops. But the only notable variation is the rice growing around Sucuá; the existence of an impermeable layer of rock a short distance below the surface is one of the physical factors, in addition to temperature, affecting the quality of rice grown. Yields reach more than 3,000 pounds per acre.

Experimental farms in the area also are influencing the crops grown. The new cattle-breeding unit near Macas has been in operation only for a short time and thus has had little effect so far. The experimental crop station on the edge of Sucuá, testing for the crops best suited to the Upano Valley, has led to the introduction of soybeans by the more innovative farmers of Sucuá. Farmers in the Macas area have not yet begun to sow soybeans. Another example is the type of grass grown for pasture: the majority of farmers around Sucuá grow *elefante* grass which can support one head of cattle per acre, but the extension agent in Macas estimates that farmers there sow 95 per cent of their pastures in *gramalote*, the traditional native pasture, which supports no more than one and one-half head per two acres.[4]

The lack of migrants to Macas is reflected in the high percentage of families having a minimum of fifteen or twenty head of cattle. But the long residence of the colonos is not the only reason for the relative prosperity. The arrival of an agency of the Banco de Fomento within the last ten years has allowed many of the poorer families to acquire cattle and to close partially the economic gap between themselves and the wealthier families. Sucuá is different in this respect because of the constant immigration of families. They do not have the means to buy cattle when they first arrive. The same problem applies to landholding. Macas, with native-born colonos, has few landless families; holdings are usually seventy-five acres or more. Smaller holdings are characteristic of Sucuá and the area between Macas and Sucuá.

As a result of immigration to the Sucuá area, farm labor is available. These recent immigrants want to earn money to acquire their own land and cattle. Thus, more labor-intensive crops can be grown, although lack of markets discourages this type of production. A major problem in Macas, according to the colonos, is the lack of labor. Previously, Jíbaros tended cattle and cleared land. The mission, in the last five years, has separated these Indians from the colonos so that they would leave their nomadic way of life for one of land and cattle ownership. Lack of labor is reflected in the comparatively high daily wage of 83 cents to $1.38, plus meals. The laborer in the Sierra earns around 55 cents per day. Another reflection of labor scarcity is the lack of vegetables, a labor-intensive crop. Peas, tomatoes, and other vegetables are flown in from time to time. Even wood for cooking is expensive—an incongruity, with so much forest—because of the scarcity of labor.

The Proyecto de Colonización del Valle del Río Upano estimates that 23 per cent of the people in the Upano Valley are engaged in commerce and 14 per cent in artisanship. Macas may show such percentages, but in addition to running a store, a family will also have land and cattle. Sucuá shows the same division of employment, but fewer people engage in both commerce and cattle raising.

Sucuá, with increasing numbers of migrants and more activity,

4. An exception to the use of gramalote for pasture in the Macas zone is a German immigrant who has been in the zone for fifteen years. His 225 acres of pasture are in elefante.

has more problems with thievery than Macas, a less dynamic place where everybody knows everybody else and what possessions each family has. Repayment of loans is no problem in Macas either— even the formerly seminomadic Jíbaros repay them.

Many variables enter into the differences between the two towns, only thirteen miles apart. What will happen in the future has been suggested. The determining factor will be a penetration road. The effects will be far-reaching and will probably change Macas more than Sucuá, since it has to make a greater adjustment to the in- creased circulation and traffic that the road is certain to bring. What erosion to the traditional ways of life in Macas, which have survived over 350 years, will occur?

Eastward from Zamora.—The road from Loja to Zamora has not penetrated farther eastward toward the area claimed by both Ecua- dor and Peru; until the boundary dispute is settled to the satisfaction of both the governments, development in the disputed area will certainly be minimal.

OVERVIEW

It has been impossible over the years to get a national effort behind the construction of a few but significant penetration roads into the Oriente; rather the residents of each *municipio* or county have tried to get national funds for the construction of a road from their own locality to the east. When such funds are not forthcoming, or are spent on other road projects, local residents and their leaders are no longer interested. For instance, there is an ungraveled, fair- weather road that leads from Latacunga across the highlands to the east; as it descends on the eastern flank of the cordillera it becomes a trail. Regional leaders in Latacunga spend much time and energy on making this trail into a road. They are not at all interested in helping pay the costs of road building eastward from Quito, or from Ambato, or from any other center of the Sierra. And it is re- ported that the people of Ambato have steadfastly opposed the efforts to improve the Quito-Papallacta road, especially its extension to Tena via Baeza, because they fear that products from Tena would then flow to the Quito market rather than to Ambato.

By way of contrast, brief mention might be made of western Ecuador. The 27,000-odd square miles of coastal Ecuador produce a large exportable surplus of bananas, coffee, cacao, rice, sugar, cotton, citrus fruits, and pineapples. In fact this is the most fertile and promising part of the country—and one of the most fertile and promising rainy tropical lowlands in the Western Hemisphere—provided, again, that transport facilities are improved. Thousands of acres of these forestlands are well suited to crops and pastures. *Santo Domingo de los Colorados*—A vast new area *west* of the Andes was opened up for agriculture with the completion of the road from Quito to Santo Domingo de los Colorados in 1947 and beyond to Esmeraldas in 1949. The government has already settled about 1,600 families on 420,000 acres of land and is planning the settlement of another 4,400 families. The soils are fertile, average temperatures range between 75 and 79, rainfall is between 60 and 80 inches a year, and there is no dry season. Here bananas, cacao, and coffee are grown for the domestic market in Quito. Thousands of independent banana farms, mostly small holdings of 10 to 30 acres, many of them owned by Negros, now line this road northward from Santo Domingo to Esmeraldas. A sine qua non for comparable favorable results of efforts at colonization and agricultural development *east* of the Andes is the construction of all-weather penetration roads and making land available for the land hungry.

REFERENCES: ECUADOR

Barrueco, Domingo. *Historia de Macas.* Quito: Centro Misional de Investigaciones Científicas, 1959.
Beghin, Francisco Javier. "Condiciones de servidumbre vigentes en las haciendas del Oriente ecuatoriano." *Planificación* 1, no. 2 (Mayo 1963):81–99.
Brunori, Pier G. "La provincia Morona-Santiago nell'oriente equatoriano, con particolare reguardo alle vallate Upano-Namangoza e Zamora." *Revisti di Agricultura Subtropicale e Tropicale* 54, nos. 1–3 (Gennaio–Marzo 1960): 54–72.
Burt, Arthur L., et al. "Santo Domingo de los Colorados—A New Pioneer Zone in Ecuador." *Economic Geography* 36, no. 3 (July 1960):221–30.
Casagrande, J. B., et al. "Colonization as a Research Frontier: The Ecuadorian Case." In *Process and Pattern in Culture,* edited by Robert Alan Manners. Chicago: Aldine Publishing Co., 1964.
Cisneros Cisneros, César. "Indian Migrations from the Andean Zone of Ecuador to the Lowlands." *América Indígena* 19, no. 3 (July 1959):226–43.
Comité Interamericano de Desarrollo Agrícola. *Tenencia de la tierra y desarrollo socio-económico del sector agrícola: Ecuador.* Washington: Pan American Union, 1965.
Conforti, Emilio. "Posibilidades económicas para la introducción de nuevos cultivos en el Ecuador." *Planificación* 1, no. 1 (Septiembre-Diciembre 1962) : 122–47.
Ecuador. Centro de Reconversión Económica del Azuay, Cañar y Morona-Santiago. *Projecto de colonización del Valle del Río Upano.* Cuenca, 1964.
———. Instituto Ecuatoriano de Reforma Agraria y Colonización. *Estadísticas de las realizaciones en reforma agraria y colonización.* Quito, 1968.

Hansis, Richard. "Colonization in the Upano River Valley, Ecuador." Master's thesis, University of Florida, 1968.

Holloway, H. L. "East of the Ecuadorian Andes." *Geographical Journal* 80, no. 5 (November 1932):410–19.

Jaramillo Alvarado, Pío. *Las provincias orientales del Ecuador: exámen histórico-administrativo.* Quito: Editorial Casa de la Cultura Ecuatoriana, 1964.

López Córdovez, Luis Alberto. *Zonas agrícolas del Ecuador.* Quito: Junta Nacional de Planificación, 1961.

Navarro Andrade, Ulpiano, *Geografía económica del Ecuador.* Quito: Editorial Santo Domingo, 1966.

Porras Garcés, Pedro Ignacio. *Contribución al estudio de la arqueología e historia de los Valles Quijos y Misagualli (Alto Napo) en la región oriental del Ecuador, S.A.* Quito: Editora Fenix, 1961.

Rassmuss, Juan E. "Oil Development Starts in Ecuador's Amazon Basin." *World Petroleum* (February 1968), p. 12.

5. Peru

In the Peru of the early 1930s, the Andean highlands and the Oriente were connected by only a few routes, notably the Pichis Trail—from the Central Highlands to the Pichis River, headstream of the Pachitea, tributary of the upper Ucayali River—and the more northerly route from Cajamarca to Yurimaguas. Even when supplemented by aviation and radio communications, such laborious travel routes were not enough to hold the nation together. In 1932, it took Earl Parker Hanson, explorer and geographer, two months to go from Iquitos to Lima via the Northern Trail, "an elapsed time that was fine for detailed studies and observations but not for the management of a modern nation. In those days people who had to travel between the capital and Iquitos still tried, if they had the money, to go by steamer via the Panama Canal and the Amazon River, at times with convenient stopovers in Paris."[1] Political turbulence in Peru's "Wild East" finally convinced the national government that something had to be done to hold the nation together. One result was the establishment of a naval base near Iquitos; another result, far more important, was the construction of the first of Peru's "access" roads from the Pacific coastal plain over the Andes to navigable Amazonian waterways. In the early 1940s, the road from Lima reached Tingo María on the Huallaga River, today a thriving frontier town with a population of about 8,000, a significant producer of tea and coca leaves. From there construction continued toward the east until, in 1943, the road reached Pucallpa on the Ucayali River.

Flying a northeast course out of Lima's Jorge Chávez International Airport, one follows a panorama of natural divisions until disembarking in Pucallpa an hour later. First in view is the narrow

1. "New Conquistadors in the Amazon Jungle," p. 2.

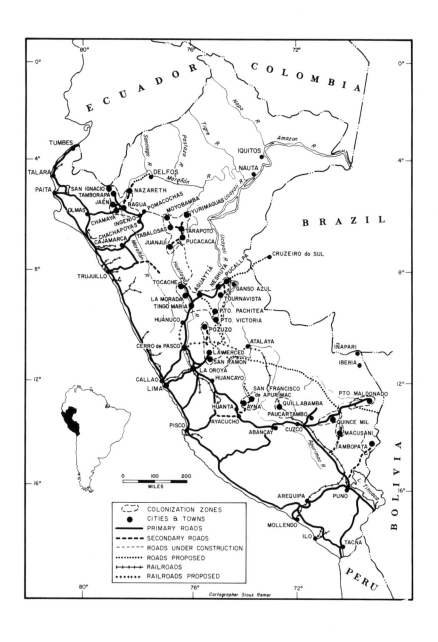

coastal lowland of closely spaced alluvial fans, an extremely arid desert except where irrigated fields of cotton and sugarcane are interrupted by rocky spurs from the Andes. There is a steady climb in altitude until the leveling of the craft displays rows of towering peaks (the highest between 18,000 and 20,000 feet above sea level) with pellucid lakes and glacial moraines. These gradually give way to a more uniform surface of gentle slopes and broad valleys traversed by the tributaries of the Amazon on their journey northward and eastward. This surface eventually disappears into a "mountain forest" of small trees and deep, steep-sided canyons with vertical rock walls—the rainy, cold *ceja de la montaña,* or "eyebrow of the forest."

Beyond lies the montaña proper. After the plane passes over the forested foothills of the Andes (about 3,000 feet in elevation), the slope merges with the selva, or tropical rain forest. A few low hills break the flatness of the country until these last outposts of the Andes open onto the Pampa del Sacramento, a tropical forested plain. A flight of an additional 130 miles over an unbroken mantle of green ends at the busy commercial hub of Pucallpa, approximately 50,000 population, several miles to the west of the meandering course of the Ucayali River.

The montaña of Peru, which includes more than 60 per cent of the national territory and has less than 10 per cent of the population, began to receive attention during the presidency of Ramón Castilla (1845–51) who formulated plans for the settlement and development of the east. Not until the government of President Benavides (1931–39) were the first roads of penetration into the montaña initiated.[2] In 1943 the easternmost extension of the Trans-Andean Highway was officially opened by President Prado, who, with a retinue of cars, made the trip from Lima to the Ucayali. This marked the completion of the first road of penetration into the Peruvian montaña that reaches the navigable waters of the Amazon River system. For the first time water-borne cargo from its numerous tributaries could be transshipped and sent to highland and coastal markets by relatively cheap truck transportation.[3]

After crossing the last range that parallels the Andean front (the Cordillera Azul), the central Trans-Andean Highway penetrates the

2. Emilio Delboy, "Memorandum sobre la selva del Perú," p. 9.
3. Wolfram U. Drewes, *The Economic Development of the Western Montaña of Central Peru as Related to Transportation,* p. 20.

undulating, tropical forested plains of the Amazon Basin. The road follows the low divide between two major tributaries of the Río Ucayali, the Aguaytia and Pachitea rivers. The divide is broken up by minor tributaries, and alluvial landforms are the dominant characteristics of the region. Rivers meander and often have no definitive course. Important trace minerals are often lacking in the leached tropical soils. Large areas of low land are inundated during the annual flood season. As a result, settlement has been concentrated along the road and also on the higher river banks and on dry alluvial terraces unaffected by the fluctuation of the river level.[4]

Although the Tingo María–Pucallpa road (178 miles) was completed in 1943, connecting the Peruvian Amazon Basin with Lima, it was many years before the land along the road began to be cropped by squatters and peasant proprietors. Even today the cropped area reaches back only a few hundred yards from the road. In the beginning, emphasis was on the usual subsistence crops, such as corn, beans, yuca, and bananas, but increasingly farmers are turning to tree crops, as the markets for them develop; further, they have found that under such ecological conditions, perennials maintain their yields much better than shallow rooted annuals. Good prices for bananas have been a special incentive to small-scale producers.

Cropping practices differ greatly from place to place and from crop to crop, depending on the background and capacity of individual cultivators. The coca bushes on the steep slopes in the vicinity of Tingo María are a prey to erosion caused by torrential rains. The growers, for the most part poor, illiterate, and unskilled, practice clean cultivation of their plots, thus promoting erosion.

In marked contrast are the tea plantations a few miles away along the Tingo María–Pucallpa highway; these are operated by second-generation Peruvians of Japanese ancestry who have capital and know-how and are able to employ the most modern techniques of production and processing. Their lands are not eroding.

PIONEER SETTLEMENT

Robert C. Eidt has made a significant contribution to the study of pioneer settlement in eastern Peru,[5] in historical perspective, dis-

---

4. Ibid.
5. "Pioneer Settlement in Eastern Peru."

The soil of this small coca plantation near Tingo María in eastern Peru is being rapidly eroded. Farmers are clearing small plots on the steep mountain slopes beyond the town.

Air view of a well-managed tea plantation about ten miles from Tingo María on the road to Pucallpa. Only the road cut is eroding.

cussing the roles of the church, the government, and private entrepreneurs.

Incorporation of the montaña, or the Oriente as it was sometimes
called, within the Spanish orbit was a task assumed by the early
Spanish conquerors, with the dual hope of finding El Dorado and
containing Portuguese westward expansion. But it was found that
the forest Indians were hostile, communications were difficult, supplies were not easy to obtain, and little gold was to be found. As a
result, the Spaniards did not remain anywhere in the montaña in
significant numbers, and the main task of the reduction and settlement of Indians in this area was turned over by the Crown to the
Franciscan Order. Missions and mule trails were established; hundreds of families of forest Indians were gradually settled around
these missions, or *reducciones*, where they were indoctrinated with
Christianity at the same time that they were instructed in agricultural techniques; mission farm products, including the first pigs
and chickens, were exchanged for salt, tropical fruits, and Indian
labor.

In the neighborhood of Quimirí (La Merced), on upland western
tributaries of the Ucayali River, Indians had long mined salt at
Cerro de la Sal along the Paucartambo River. Later, deposits of
gold, silver, and iron were discovered; these finds attracted lay
Spanish settlers, but there was so much quarreling among them that
the viceroy soon stopped all colonization activities.

In 1686 the Franciscans reached an agreement with the Jesuits,
by which the former were restricted to parts of the montaña above
1,000 feet elevation. This restriction contributed to the successes the
friars achieved in areas where living conditions were comfortable
and malaria less of a problem than north of the Marañón. Reducciones were created in the central montaña, Pangoa and Pozuzo
(1709–13). In 1709 the Cerro de la Sal region was reopened and work
was carried on toward the Apurímac Valley. By 1730, shortly before
the Jesuits established missions in the Iquitos region, the Franciscans
had explored the Perené Basin eastward from Cerro de la Sal and
entered the desolate, inaccessible, hilly area north of the river, the
Gran Pajonal, consisting of a large number of hilltop grasslands,
openings in the forest apparently originally cleared and burned by
the Campa Indians.

Mission activity was revived during the latter part of the nineteenth century, especially on the lower Ucayali, a major route to the

Amazon. In the low-lying monotonous plains of Amazonia, average annual rainfall is around 100 inches. Here malarial mosquitoes breed by the millions in the depressions (*bajios*), temperatures and humidity are high, soils easily lose their fertility under the system of slash-and-burn agriculture, and the *japa*, or *jején* (*Ixodes* sp.), and *nigua* (*Pulex penetrans*), parasitic worms and vampire bats, add variety if not zest to tropical living. In spite of these factors, the friars continued their work on the reducciones, until the plans of the Order were upset by international events.

There was a growing market for products made of natural rubber, the most important source of which was the vast selva of South America. The demand was so great that, as early as 1880, rubber hunters were working their way from Brazil and Bolivia into eastern Peru, where they raided and frequently destroyed Indian settlements, reducciones of the Franciscans, in search of slave labor. Rebellions and uprisings were common, and friction increased between friars and laymen. In 1900 missionary operations of the Order were restricted to the central portion of the eastern lowlands, while the Dominicans assumed responsibilities in the departments of Loreto and Madre de Dios where the best (Hevea) rubber was most abundant. The latter have gradually regained the confidence of the Indians; they encourage them to settle permanently around the mission outposts, and they continue to make valuable contributions to the knowledge of eastern Peru in such places as Iberia, Puerto Esperanza, and Quincemil.

Government colonization projects in the montaña have been carried on in a most haphazard and uncoordinated manner. In 1857 the Peruvian government selected 300 immigrant families in Germany—people anxious to avoid wars, conscription laws, and land shortages—and paid their passage to Lima. The colonists were to be established at intervals along the proposed transport link between costa and montaña. But when they reached Peru there was not even a trail to the site of Pozuzo, where the old Franciscan mission had long since been abandoned, and where the first colony was to be located. The would-be settlers underwent terrible hardships while crossing the Andes, almost starving while crude trails were being built. Some died en route, many defected, and only half the original contingent reached their destination. Those who survived planted manioc, bananas, and beans for home use, and, later, cotton, sugarcane, tobacco, coca, and coffee as cash crops which were—and still are—exported on mule back to roadheads. In spite of the serious inroads of tropical diseases, such as malaria and yellow fever, a local water supply with harmful amounts of magnesium, and declining yields of cash crops, the colony has managed to survive. "The fact that most of the colonists were ardent Catholics and thus had common religious and social outlets, that they were family people used to cultivating rugged, forested landscapes, and that they had no desire to return to Europe or join urban residents in Lima would seem to account for their success in the face of so many obstacles."[6] In 1960 some 1,800 people of German descent lived in the Pozuzo–Puerto Victoria region, proof that persistence, resourcefulness, and hardiness make pioneering possible in the forest.

In 1864, one hundred miles south of Pozuzo, some 320 Italians settled in the vicinity of a fort established at San Ramón; they were followed by Peruvians who settled on small lots along the trail northward to La Merced at the old Franciscan mission of Quimirí. Since these colonists lacked knowledge of tropical agricultural practices and export of any surplus was prohibitively costly, most of them were in time forced to sell to Peruvians wealthy enough to consolidate holdings and engage in the large-scale production of sugarcane, coffee, cacao, and tobacco. This region has continued to tempt the small operator, often without skill or capital, with the result that much of the steeper land has been gutted by accelerated erosion as a result of uncontrolled deforestation.

Expansion of settlement in the south, where Peru had lost land to Brazil, had distinct political and strategic overtones. In the Madre de Dios region, government forces paved the way for colonists; in 1912 an expedition founded Puerto Maldonado (elevation, 845 feet) along the Bolivian border near the confluence of the Madre de Dios River and two of its tributaries. The area became known for its exceptional climate, for here the effects of low elevation are offset by cool southeast winds known as *friajes*. Windy periods (known as *surazos* in eastern Bolivia) are associated with cold fronts of storms from southern Brazil and Argentina, and offer a welcome change from the hot days. Large land grants were available to settlers; rubber and *castaña* trees (*Bertholletia excelsa*, the Brazil nut) were numerous, and gold could be panned in the rivers; the result was that people happily settled in this remote sector and established a thriving economy that has shown remarkable continuity.

6. Ibid., p. 263.

When the official central montaña road reached Tingo María in 1936, Peruvian colonists, with a handful of Europeans and Americans, began at once to develop montaña holdings, with tea and coffee among the most important crops. After the highway to Pucallpa was opened to traffic in 1943, making a large new area accessible to settlement, government colonization centers gave scientific agricultural aid, administered land grants, and organized district police protection, schools, cooperative stores, and health services. Thousands of acres of land were soon under cultivation at Tingo María and many more thousands along the road to Pucallpa, which, in view of the accessible market in Lima, soon surpassed Iquitos as the country's most important source of lumber. As a result of broad-based and long-range settlement planning, colonization along the central Trans-Andean road continues in spite of seemingly unfavorable climate and the difficulty of obtaining a clear land title.

There are other transportation-colonization projects in the Oriente: the Cuzco-Quincemil highway, completed in 1943, and later extended to Puerto Maldonado; the extension in 1961 of the Valle de la Convención railroad to the montaña town of Quillabamba; the Ayacucho-Ayna link with the Apurímac; and the Puno-Tambopata project.

Difficulties with Colombia and Ecuador have required the maintenance of Peruvian security forces along the northern montaña border and have retarded civilian settlement in that zone. Small army outposts have been built along the boundary, where land grants are of necessity restricted to "acceptable" citizens. Military bases have also been established along the Brazilian frontier. Some 7,000 acres of army farm colonies are more or less self-supporting agricultural units. The army has assumed a civic role in constructing and maintaining roads and airports in the montaña. The task of making the Central Trans-Andean road from Lima to Pucallpa serviceable in all types of weather has been assigned to the army, with financial and technical aid from the Alliance for Progress.

The Peruvian Air Force has played a major role in opening up the montaña, by aiding in the transfer of many types of cargo to and from the Oriente. SATCO (Servicio Aereo de Transportes Comerciales) pilots annually bring out thousands of tons of coca, barbasco root, coffee, tea, peanuts, and other raw materials, either directly to Lima or to mountain airstrips from which trucks transport them to Lima or other consumption centers.

In 1943 the nation acquired some 15,000 acres at Iberia on the east bank of the Tahuamanu River, about 60 miles north of Puerto Maldonado, and turned it over to the Banco de Fomento Agropecuario (Development Bank for Agriculture and Animal Husbandry) for management. The bank organized the new farm in sections, appointed trained personnel for farming, cattle raising, and rubber collecting, and began a colonization program. Homes were constructed for workers and officials, as were a commissary, school, theater, airstrip, and sawmill.

Eleven separate 135-acre pastures were cleared from the forest, on which hundreds of cross-bred cattle (Zebu-Criollo) were soon grazing on native grasses that supported about one head per hectare, or 2.5 acres. Rice, corn, beans, and manioc were planted as staples. In 1958 the bank began the program of making 75-acre grants to *colonos*, who were required to plant crops needed by the hacienda or *fundo*. Upland or dry rice is planted on cleared forest land. After it is harvested, a second crop of beans, manioc, or corn serves as a cash crop, and then the area is turned into pasture for eight to ten years.

The Ministerio de Agricultura administers a 7,000-acre cattle ranch established in 1950 at Neshuya on the Tingo María–Pucallpa highway, to demonstrate to settlers that scientific cattle-breeding programs in the wet tropical parts of Peru can successfully supply milk and meat locally, with a surplus later for export to the mountains or the coast. The same agency has founded another cattle ranch at San Jorge near Pucallpa. Introduced *Yaragúa* (*Hyparrhenia rufa* [Nees] Stapf) and *Pará* (*Panicum purpurascens*) grasses have proved their worth, as has the viney *Kudzu* (*Pueraria thunbergiana*), relished by cattle if used when young and tender as chopped feed. Carrying capacity is five times what it is in the sierra grazing lands and production efficiency is also much higher, resulting in heavier two-year-old animals.

In 1948 an Italian-Peruvian Company (SAIPAI) received a concession of some 37,000 acres just north of Tingo María and contracted fifteen families for a three-year period. Unfortunately, few of the colonists had farm experience, yet they had to engage in hard physical labor with few of the amenities to which people are accustomed or aspire to have; further, there were no doctors, and the colony was five miles from the nearest transportation center. Only three of the settlers remained after the termination of their contracts. After 1953 the federal government allowed Peruvians to settle in the colony, which they promptly did, as squatters and on the best land available. Since it is impossible under Peruvian law to oust squatters once they have established themselves, SAIPAI is engaged in a holding action, hoping to retain control over the thousand acres originally cleared for the production of rubber, cacao, and coffee. As can be seen, the possibility of being able to exploit a large concession of land gradually, scientifically, and rationally is remote, if not actually dangerous.

By Presidential Decree of April 21, 1960, all land in the montaña region between parallels 10 and 13 south latitude and between the 75 and 72 meridians west, an area of some 45,000 square miles, was set aside for massive scientific settlement and development, under *Plan Peruvia*. This region, just east of the largest markets in the country—Cerro de Pasco, Cuzco, and Lima—is to a large extent free of the claims of large landholders and subsistence squatters. There are very good soils in many sectors; where land is level and not subject to flooding, both bananas and cacao do well and are as yet free from diseases, and a welcome and pleasant dry season lasting up to two months is experienced in many parts of the region. There are relatively concentrated stands of commercially usable timber, a natural focus of river transportation routes at Atalaya where the navigable Ucayali commences, and a dam site on the Mantaro River at which a hydroelectric plant will be built that will supply over 3 million kilowatts of power to the adjacent markets in the sierra and the costa.

THE APURÍMAC VALLEY

Norman Stewart, in a perceptive paper,[7] has investigated the spontaneous settlement of highland Quechua-speaking Indians in that relatively large reservoir of potentially productive land in the Apurímac Valley—within the area of Plan Peruvía. He found that the wave of migrants is rapidly increasing, that as they clear forest, plant crops, and build homes in the new site their attachment to the highlands weakens, and that they must work out their salvation in an area where land is already in part occupied by native Indian subsistence farmers and by extensive *latifundia*.

The Campa, the tropical forest tribe of the vicinity, are gradually being either enticed or coerced into the plantation labor supply,

7. "Migration and Settlement in the Peruvian Montaña: The Apurímac Valley."

or retreating farther into the forest as population increases and wildlife becomes less abundant. The best croplands in the valley are monopolized by the latifundia for the commercial production of coca, barbasco, cacao, coffee, and bananas. For most highlanders (*serranos*), the haciendas are an important link in the transition from migrant to independent agricultural pioneer, for, after gaining valuable experience in tropical agriculture on the haciendas, they move as squatters to some remote corner of the property. All serranos, besides growing subsistence crops of manioc, maize, beans, cotton and bananas, produce coca and barbasco for the market; they have been able to speed up commercial production by extensive use of cooperative labor.

The importance of the Apurímac settlement is such that it has received official notice: "The character of Apurímac settlement and its implications for the development of the montaña have recently attracted official attention. In the last three years the Peruvian government has approached the problem in several ways. Of direct concern is the decision by the Institute of Agrarian Reform and Colonization to attempt the systematic reorganization of serrano settlement in the Apurímac Valley. On the basis of surveys conducted in 1961–62, most of the gently sloping land on the right bank of the river was selected as the site of a planned agricultural colony. Expropriation procedures are under way, and farms and a townsite have been surveyed. Serranos in the area will be provided with credit for the purchase of eighty-acre parcels; an experimental farm and social, educational, and medical amenities are planned. The project is frankly experimental: the reservoir of planning experience is not great, and the serranos themselves are skeptical and suspicious of government intentions."[8]

Further, here is proof that the highland Indian can readily adjust to the tropical environment: "By their migrations to the Apurímac the highland Quechua have refuted the generally accepted notion that they are repelled by, or cannot function within, the tropical forest. The serranos have voluntarily accepted the challenges of an entirely different habitat and have experienced remarkably little difficulty in reorienting their culture patterns to fit their new circumstances. The process by which they have made these adjustments invite systematic analysis by cultural geographers, but

8. Ibid., p. 156.

traditional conservatism does not appear to function as a barrier to successful montaña settlement."[9]

Professor Stewart concludes that, "The colonization of the Apurímac, and the larger development schemes of which it is a part, represent important steps toward solution of the interrelated problems of population maldistribution and expansion of the effective national territory to Peru's international boundaries. Settlement of the montaña cannot be viewed as a substitute for land reform or intensification of agriculture in the sierra. Selva migration, even when organized and facilitated, is at best gradual. However, along the Apurímac the serrano has demonstrated a capacity for successful tropical-forest pioneering. If such settlement can be encouraged and stabilized, Peru may yet win the struggle to accommodate its burgeoning population at an acceptable standard of living."[10]

YURIMAGUAS-TARAPOTO AREA

On the San Ramón plantation, a few miles out of Yurimaguas in the northern montaña, on landholdings totaling some 75,000 acres and owned by the Lima firm of Domingo Loero y Cía, another important development is occurring. The plantation resulted from the World War II activities of Domingo Loero Sr., who scoured the dense jungles for rubber and decided that the land could be put to better uses than that of merely producing one widely scattered industrial raw material. His firm has now cleared some 12,000 acres of land on which it maintains a herd of beef cattle. It has also been very successful with rice, which is in desperately short supply in Peru. So far only upland rice is produced, but there are plans to experiment with wet rice. A large rice mill works steadily on the plantation, augmenting the nation's food supplies and turning out improved seeds for distribution throughout the Amazonian regions. In the Yurimaguas area, upland rice is produced by over 1,000 families on 10,000 acres. The new firm, Arrocera del Huallaga S.A., a joint effort of Peruvian and Texas rice growers, has begun preliminary work on the auxiliary construction of a modern rice-processing plant; it was to have been completed by mid-1969, with an initial milling and storage capacity of 16,000 metric tons of rice a year. Capacity may be doubled should increased rice production in the Yurimaguas area warrant it.

9. Ibid., p. 154.
10. Ibid., p. 157.

The San Ramón plantation is a large operation requiring machinery and capital; the company's policies differ greatly from those of many of the traditional large landowners throughout South America. It cooperates with the government in agricultural experimentation. It also welcomes new settlers, including Indian squatters who drift into the forested parts of its land, and Brazilians who have fled from the recurring climatic disasters in their country's Northeast. Further, the company helps such settlers to get started on its lands, sets them up to plant rice and other crops, and buys their produce. Until the company has recovered its investment in them, the new settlers are sharecroppers, but the aim is to help them become independent landowners producing rice, beef, pork, chickens, palm oil, Manila hemp, and the other crops Peru needs. Yet the Oriente program has had relatively little success with people from other parts of Peru. People from the highlands and the dry valleys along the Pacific coast tend to dislike the humid tropical climate so much that about 80 per cent of them return shortly after their arrival.

The new road, which runs 84 miles southwest from Yurimaguas to Tarapoto, was opened in October 1964. Today it is an extremely busy thoroughfare over which Tarapoto's needs are supplied and its crops of coffee, tobacco, and cotton are taken out. The present flow of traffic between Lima and Tarapoto, with its rich agricultural surroundings, is primarily as follows: from Lima to Pucallpa by truck; from Pucallpa down the Ucayali River to Iquitos or Nauta by boat; then, also by boat, up the Marañón and Huallaga rivers to Yurimaguas; from Yurimaguas by truck to Tarapoto. However, a new highway from the Pacific eastward is now moving with aggravating slowness toward Tarapoto.

The Northern Trans-Andean Highway connecting the coastal towns of Trujillo and Chiclayo to Pomacocha has been completed, but Tarapoto will not have a highway connection to the coast until the road across 150 kilometers of rough, heavily forested terrain between Pomacocha and Rioja has been built.

Within the past few decades, Tarapoto's population has grown from 5,000 to 30,000; the growth promises to be spectacular when the highway reaches the city. Perhaps Tarapoto will be for Peru's East what Omaha, Nebraska, has long been for the United States West. From Tarapoto southward, the Ministry of Public Works is now energetically building a new road toward Tingo María, there to tie in with the Lima-Pucallpa road and to form an important section of the Venezuela-Bolivia forest edge highway (Carretera Marginal de la Selva). When that road is completed, Tarapoto will be in direct overland contact with the capital and will be able to eliminate the present 600-mile river trip via the Huallaga, Marañón, and Ucayali rivers to the roadhead at Pucallpa.

Pucallpa and Vicinity

Situated on a high river bank (495 feet above sea level) 524 miles from Lima, at the eastern terminus of the Central Trans-Andean Highway, Pucallpa is the commercial center of the Bajo Ucayali. This town of 50,000 inhabitants has shown an astonishing increase in population. In 1915 it contained only three small stores (*tambos*) serving a population of fifty persons who settled in expectation of a proposed railroad which never came. Boats docked "porque en ese lugar podían proveerse de ganado vacuno o porcino."[11] By 1922 these shops were abandoned and Juan Coriat dryly commented "no se encontraba ningún ser viviente a excepción de los insectos." In 1926 this same author-traveler was denied a visit to Pucallpa, for the launch captain asserted it was one of the poorest sites along the Ucayali and refused him permission to disembark. A desultory living could still be earned by tapping wild rubber in the forests where the Shipibo Indians lived their typical wild jungle existence and occasionally made war on other Indians or white men. For transportation, Pucallpans had to depend almost exclusively on balsa rafts, dugout canoes, and occasional launches which went down the Ucayali to Iquitos.

On a return trip in 1932, Coriat found quite a change. The town now contained an airport built by the government in its attempt to open the montaña, linking Pucallpa with Iquitos to the north and with San Ramón to the south. By 1940, 397 families totaling 2,368 persons inhabited Pucallpa, which now harbored the marks of its growth from village to town—plaza, casino, and electric lights. Since the 1940 census and three decades since the completion of the road, the population has increased more than twenty-one-fold.

The Pucallpa of today is a modern frontier city with water, sewerage, electric services, and streets, and scattered sidewalks which the slightest downpour will turn into a morass of slippery mud. Houses

11. Juan E. Coriat, *El hombre del Amazonas y ensayo monográfico de Loreto*, p. 171.

and buildings often have the appearance of hastily built, temporary structures, with thatch roofs and reed sides. It has schools, hospitals, banks, theaters, hotels, numerous commercial establishments from Singer stores to the ubiquitous ice popsicle stands, and hundreds of trucks, cars, motorcycles, and scooters. The major industries include sixteen sawmills, four rice mills, and three rosewood oil factories. Commercial production in the Plywood Peruana S.A. plant began in 1966 and Ganso Azul, a Sinclair subsidiary, completed a 2,500 b/d refining plant in 1967 for its producing fields nearby. Of lesser importance are the cola bottling plant, ice plant, and brick factory.

It is in the activity along the streets, in commercial house and café, that Pucallpa differs from other montaña settlements. There is the distant hum of a sawmill, the occasional cloud of dust from a coughing jeep or the rattle as bumper unexpectedly meets road, the regular staccato of horse and mule hoofbeats as they head for the polluted river (the source of water for those houses without it) laden with four one-gallon tin containers, the grating sound of an ice crusher as a barefooted youngster waits for his *chupete* (flavored ice), the 5 to 8 A.M. shuffling parade to the outdoor market, where oranges, bananas, papayas, watermelons, olives, tomatoes, potatoes, yams, onions, grilled monkeys, turtles, fish, chickens, ducks, turtle eggs, corn, bread, and grains adorn the weather-beaten stands, the occasional stench arising from the "campo libre" bathroom facilities, the bearded adventurer selling every bird or animal the jungle offers him, and the cautious step of the missionary wife.

The activity along Pucallpa's river front creates another atmosphere of commercial movement. It is here that the forest products are collected for transshipment to the sierra and coastal markets, here that the supplier of this market docks and lives on his combination houseboat and cargo ship while plying the Ucayali, here that the canoes anchor as they transport local products to early morning market, here that the sawmills, the rosewood oil factories, and the petroleum storage plant receive their raw materials, here a group of people live in thatched, stilted huts, and here occasionally a family of Shipibo Indians is encamped on the shore, roasting *plátanos* under a makeshift shelter and selling their handicraft before disappearing into the jungle.

Pucallpa is destined to become the St. Louis of Peru's "Wild East." The road from there to Lima is now paved and one can drive across Peru in twelve hours at any time of year. Along the road new enterprises have sprung up in recent years. A Swiss is finding the production of chickens and eggs profitable; Booth Lines is creating a plantation to produce cashew nuts; rubber groves have been planted and Manila hemp is being produced in increasing quantities. There are plans for a cannery for pineapple juice.

Not far from Pucallpa is the large million-acre Tournavista enterprise, started in 1954 as a mission project by the United States LeTourneau earth-moving equipment concern. The company was systematically cutting out all commercially valuable hardwood trees, then bringing in its huge machines to push over the remaining trees; after burning, pasture grasses were planted and the land stocked with cattle. The management was concerned with large-scale lumber and beef production at the time it was taken over by the reform-minded Alvarado government. Emphasis in the future will be placed on making small plots of land available for farmers who will engage in small-scale, mixed farming activities.

The Albert Schweitzer Amazon Hospital near Pucallpa, founded in 1960 by a German-born, naturalized Peruvian doctor, is a badly needed, modest, but growing institution. Precariously financed by foundations and private individuals, it is chronically understaffed, but is already a haven for those suffering from diseases such as tuberculosis, tropical anemia, skin ulcers, and intestinal parasites. The victims of these diseases and infestations are usually unaware of their malaise, and even if they do know the causes of their health problems they have nothing with which to pay for medicines and care. Even relatively inexpensive antimalarial specifics cannot be bought on a zero income. Small wonder that it is estimated that four out of five Indian children die before adolescence. Every effort is being made to teach the forest dwellers how to avoid infection in the first place by training them in rudimentary nursing, infant care, and general practice of aesepsis. Further, it is hoped that if they learn gardening and animal husbandry, they will be able to overcome dietary deficiencies and thus be less susceptible to disease.

A few miles from Pucallpa at the settlement of Yarinacocha, on the forest-clad banks of the ox-bow lake Yarinacocha, an abandoned channel of the meandering Ucayali, is located the Summer Institute of Linguistics, a mission organization supported financially by various religious institutions and by the University of Oklahoma. Well equipped with a fleet of planes, the institute can reach almost any jungle river and settlement in a short time. The members of the staff serve a vast jungle area where they learn and record the languages of the Indian tribes to whom they at the same time bring the Word. But the institute is interested in the total man, and Indians are taught hygiene, agriculture, animal husbandry, and community development. It has already built up a herd of over forty dairy cows to be given to those Indians who are able to take care of them. Malnutrition is endemic among the jungle Indians, and campaigns that will result in their increased use of protective foods will save many lives. Institutions such as this school and the Schweitzer Hospital are in short supply, but they are a beginning and their influence will snowball. They are instrumental in greatly reducing the death rate, particularly the rate of infant mortality, among those already living in the Oriente, thus favoring more rapid population growth in situ.

A new settlement of Shipibo Indians, created by the government within its program for assimilating the primitive forest Indians, has also been located near Pucallpa. It is a typical jungle settlement of thatched houses, in which the women make and decorate pottery, paint on or weave into textiles the beautiful, traditional geometric Shipibo patterns, and also decorate arrows. The sturdiest structures in the village are the church and the school, built by the Indians themselves and lavishly adorned with their tribal patterns. A Shipibo, trained by the Institute of Linguistics, is the school teacher. A young agronomist is teaching the people modern agricultural techniques so they will be less dependent on hunting and gathering. It is planned that a home economics teacher will move in to teach them how to prepare vegetables and to give lessons in hygiene and dietetics.

The Shipibo realize that there is money in raising beef cattle. They are completing a road—the Indians donate their labor while the government provides surveys, supervision, tools, and machinery —to tie in with the one at Yarinacocha, some nine miles away, over which they can drive cattle to the Pucallpa market. When the road is completed the Indians will clear land, plant it to pasture grasses under the agronomist's direction, and stock it with cattle. They will obtain the animals from the government's Agricultural Bank, which will recoup principal and interest from the first two generations of calves, the third and all subsequent generations to belong to the forest Indians who, hopefully, will now be aspiring stockmen.

Anyone who would understand the promise of this area should visit the home of Joseph Hocking, in Yarinacocha. He is an American missionary who has spent over three decades in the wild Peruvian east, who has reared a family of five there, and who has shown that it is possible to tame the selva and indeed to make a good living doing so. Mr. Hocking's specialties are his chicken farm and his fruit orchard; he raises chickens and sells eggs in the Pucallpa market, as well as at the Institute, and his mangoes, grapefruit, and oranges command high prices. He was even voted mayor of the town for a two-year term and is much sought after for advice on regional and national matters as well as for help with potential farmers. It is regrettable that there are not more Mr. Hockings in the pioneer front of tropical settlement.

IQUITOS

In 1814 Iquitos, on the Marañón River, was a village of 80 people; even by 1864, the official founding date of the town, there were only 500 residents. By 1876 there was a total of 2,000. When the rubber boom collapsed, many trading posts and mushroom settlements along the rivers of Loreto and Madre de Dios Provinces declined in importance or even disappeared. But Iquitos continued to expand by virtue of its excellent site and extremely favorable location, so that it has become the largest city in the Peruvian montaña, with some 70,000 to 80,000 permanent residents, including those in the floating village of Belem.

Throughout Peru's eastern montaña regions, even in the remotest settlements with no road facilities whatever, President Belaúnde Terry (1963–68) used all the human resources at his disposal, governmental as well as civic, to push a strong integrated program for development and improvement of human life. At the naval base a few miles out of Iquitos, in the various shops (sawmill, carpenter, machine, welding), boys from Iquitos are given employment and the opportunity to learn trades. The base maintains a floating drydock. River gunboats of 300–400 tons displacement are in service for the Civic Action Program (Plan de Ayuda Cívica Militar).

Since August 1963, one gunboat has at all times been on patrol on one of the many rivers of the Province of Loreto; at times three have been out at once, on voyages lasting fifteen days. Carrying doctors and dentists furnished by the Ministry of Health, they visit isolated hamlets and the widely dispersed settlements on the river where the Ministry of Health does not maintain a permanent station. With the Air Force standing by at Iquitos to evacuate emergency cases for hospitalization, they attend, treat, and vaccinate thousands of people who previously have had no medical services whatever. The navy also brings them school teachers and teaching materials, carries their mail, and shows them motion pictures on cultural, agricultural, and health subjects. It also prepares socioeconomic reports on the wilderness regions visited, pinpoints problems, drafts plans for development, prepares progress reports.

Not only government officials but the civilian populations as well caught the Belaúnde fever. Even in the remotest hamlets, people are donating their labor to build schools. These are often primitive structures of poles and palm thatch, the best often erected by the artistic and energetic Shipibo Indians. But, primitive or not, there are schools where none had existed before. The government provides teachers and teaching materials, and over the entrance to each school hangs Peru's coat of arms and the imprint of the Ministry of Education.

Today, modern methods and machinery also are used with success. On projects maintained by the government and by private organizations, thousands of acres have been cleared of forests, with the help of machinery. After the trees are burned, the land is planted to pangola or other suitable forage grasses, and then stocked with cattle which feed on the grasses, refertilize the land, and inhibit the emergence of second-growth jungle. With the nation still short an estimated seven million animals to be self-sufficient in beef, cattle culture is spreading in the montaña region. Bulls, calves, and breeding cows are flown over the Andes from other parts of Peru as rapidly as the jungles are cleared and the pastures prepared. Hundreds of such animals have been flown all the way from Texas, while semen for artificial insemination is now sent to Peru's Amazon regions from Florida. Some of the beef is frozen and flown over the Andes to Lima. There is very little trouble from ticks; an energetic campaign of vaccination controls *aftosa*, or hoof-and-mouth disease; there seem to be few, if any, other cattle diseases.

Hogs do equally well. Manila hemp, of which the nation still imports large and growing tonnages, thrives and is cultivated in increasing quantities. Imported dwarf African oil palms are being distributed for cultivation to supply much-needed edible oils and raw materials for the nation's growing plastics industry. Near Yurimaguas, on the Huallaga River, dwarf coconut palms, some eight feet high, with nuts growing just above ground level, yield up to ninety nuts per year.

Jungle towns, which until recently had depended almost exclusively on balsa rafts and other river craft for transportation, now have landing strips for airplanes, even though the central government has had difficulty in borrowing money for their construction. The Air Force also has been pulled into the Civic Action Program. It flies a bulldozer from place to place as needed and uses civilian labor, which is often given free or in return for meals, to carve seventeen airstrips out of the forest in the Peruvian montaña. Another of its projects provides inexpensive air passenger service to areas ignored by private companies as commercially unfeasible or where additional air transportation is needed; charges are minimal, hardly covering the cost of fuel. An airborne dispensary (an Iquitos-based C–47), a joint project of the Air Force and the Ministry of Public Health, provides medical and dental services to towns with airstrips.

The Carretera Marginal de la Selva and Other Roads

In October 1963, Peru's visionary president, Fernando Belaúnde Terry, met with the Ministers of Public Works of Colombia, Ecuador, and Bolivia to discuss and plan his twentieth-century version of the Inca highway system that interconnected the old empire. "Instead of going through the middle of the unhealthful, lowland tropical rainforest, it would skirt the edge of that 'green hell' by taking a path somewhere upstream on the rivers; here, because of the altitude, the land would offer climatic and ecological advantages despite the tropical latitudes."[12] This 3,500-mile span, the Marginal Forest Highway, would hug the eastern slopes of the Andes from Colombia's border with Venezuela to Santa Cruz, Bolivia, linking with Venezuela's highways to the north and with Bolivia's railroads to southern Brazil and to Argentina. It would open up the "high jungle" to settlement and provide access to the vast Amazon river system, "increasing the best lands on the basis of technical studies of climate and agricultural potential."[13] This

12. Fernando Belaúnde Terry, *Peru's Own Conquest*, p. 162.
13. Ibid., p. 159.

north-south highway would join the twenty-four east-west penetration roads now in existence across the Andes.

Prepared by a New York engineering firm and financed by a loan from the Inter-American Development Bank and a similar amount from the four interested nations, a reconnaissance report was presented to the Joint Commission at a ceremony in the Government Palace, Lima, on April 9, 1965: the highway's estimated overall cost was U.S. $351 million; an additional U.S. $143 million for construction of feeder roads and facilities for the 1.5 millon colonists who could be settled in a 17.8-million-acre zone of immediate influence sliced out of the selva and whose agricultural production would be valued at U.S. $83 million annually. The Director of the Survey stated, "Peru could complete the construction of its [980 miles] of new highway in the year 1979, at a cost of U.S. $172 million for the highway and U.S. $56 million for colonization. The immediate zone of influence is estimated at 4,942,000 acres accommodating 500,000 colonists with an annual agricultural production of U.S. $29 million." And so Peru, guided by the report and receiving financial support from national and international sources, is slowly weaving a network of marginal forest highway and feeder roads, now a disjointed network groping its way into and along Peru's northern, central, and southern Oriente.

On the northern route to the Marañón from Olmos, there is a single pass, only 6,500 feet high, across the Western Cordillera, for which the Quebrada La Pilca acts as an open gate. The floor of this great gash, dry and barren, is strewn with sand, gravel, and giant boulders. On the slopes is a scattering of low, gray, gnarled algarroba trees, among which wander a few goats. Shafts of blue smoke ascend from earth-banked piles of wood and the acrid smell permeates the atmosphere, for even these precious and sparse trees are being cut and made into charcoal by the impoverished inhabitants. Toward the crest of the range, the Abra Porculla, the watershed between the Pacific and Atlantic, the valley narrows. Corn grows on narrow alluvial terraces, with here and there a banana plant. "Staircase farming" is seen in the distance: above, the greenish blue pastures; below, the patches of yellow or black plots, harvested and pastured or harvested and burned over.

Beyond the pass the Quebrada Hualabamba cuts into the barren red clay slopes, during the seven-mile course before it enters the broader valley of the Huancabamba River. Wherever the valley floor is wide enough, alfalfa fields and plots of bananas and sugar-cane create green oases. There are even some plots of unbelievably green rice seedlings. The large adobe houses, with calcimined white walls and tile roofs, are evidence of greater wealth than is to be seen to the west. Near Pucarra, American bamboo (guadua) and mango trees appear and the valley floor becomes a rich tropical garden.

At Chamaya the Huancabamba River changes its name to the Chamaya and the landscape changes abruptly; the tropical garden gives way to a desert-like landscape. Here a highway bordering rice fields branches off to the northwest, connecting Jaén with San Ignacio (population, 1,500; elevation, 4,500 feet) near the Ecuadorian border via a new reinforced concrete bridge, 230 feet long and two lanes, over the Tabaconas River near Tamborapa. Now only seasonal and badly maintained, often a long series of mudholes, this road eventually is to become a link in the Marginal Forest Highway, influencing with its 280 miles of planned feeder roads plus additional bridges, a zone of more than 2,500 square miles suitable for rice, coffee, and tobacco production and featuring extensive natural grasslands suitable for raising beef cattle.

The road eastward from Chamaya makes a wide swing to the north and then enters the valley of the Marañón. The bridge across the Marañón, nearly 800 feet long, is graceful, strong, and solid. The gray-green water disappears to the east in a deeply incised valley that is swallowed up behind the distant mountains, wrapped in a bluish haze. Perhaps this is indeed the bridge into the land of spices, the future El Dorado, which already produces cotton in Bagua, cattle in Chachapoyas, and the fine hardwoods of the eastern ranges.

Spearheaded by Peruvian army engineers, the present active road construction to the north has reached just beyond Nazareth, eventually to extend to Delfos on the Marañón below the treacherous Pongo de Manseriche. From the Pongo de Tentema toward Nazareth, one crosses the cultural frontier between the Quechua-speaking people of the sierra and the Aguarunas, the southernmost tribe of the Jíbaros. To the east the road continues to Ingenio; from Ingenio a Peruvian Army engineering battalion is extending it to the Nieva River, to be linked with the road under construction from Tarapoto. Thus, this 465-mile Northern Trans-Andean Highway will in due course become a solidly mapped line from Olmos on the Pan American Coastal Highway to the river port of Yurimaguas on the Huallaga.

Construction on the 145 miles of the Tarapoto–Nieva River all-weather section, with its twenty-two bridges, was begun in early 1966 under a U.S. $43.4 million contract awarded to a North American–Peruvian consortium. Some 14,000 tons of heavy road-building machinery for use on this road were shipped from New York and Baltimore to Belém do Pará by steamer, then off-loaded onto barges and towed 2,600 miles up the Amazon to Iquitos and another 600 miles beyond to Yurimaguas. There the machinery was unloaded and driven or hauled to Tarapoto over the all-weather, 84-mile road opened in 1964. On January 6, 1968, two years later, President Belaúnde Terry inaugurated the first section of the road—a 28-mile stretch, with a 410-foot bridge over the Mayo River; this section ties Tarapoto with the small town of Tabalosas to the west. When completed, this extension of the Northern Trans-Andean Highway, another link in the Marginal Forest Highway, will influence a population zone of 100,000 ("expected to increase to more than 500,000 within twenty-five years")[14] and will generally parallel the Mayo River Valley, an area of 875,000 acres, an estimated 525,000 of which are suitable for agriculture and livestock.

Financed by USAID and the Peruvian Government, construction with airlifted machinery began early in 1965 on a road south from Tarapoto, a road which now extends 75 miles along the Huallaga to Juanjuí, 50 miles of which form part of the Marginal Forest Highway. And just beyond Tingo María, pioneering northward, another graveled section of this highway, the Tulumayo–La Morada[15] section, was inaugurated in September 1967. Financed

14. William M. Denevan, "The Carretera Marginal de la Selva and the Central Huallaga Region of Peru," p. 441.

15. A note here on the high costs of success. La Morada, a small show-case community of over one hundred families, originated in 1960 through spontaneous migration from one of Lima's shantytowns. Granted 7,500 acres of some of the selva's most productive soils, surveyed into 100 lots of 75 acres by the government, the settlers also were provided with transportation, credit, clothing, and food. The colono now has 15 acres cleared and planted (5 acres in rubber, 5 in cacao, and 5 in subsistence crops and bananas), sowing the land first in maize for two years, then in plantains for three years, then in cacao or rubber. However, as R. F. Watters stresses in his "Shifting Cultivation in Peru," there has been a "very great degree of government [and private] assistance involved in the project, including regular technical assistance. . . . It certainly could not be supplied at this rate to a large number of other colonization schemes." He continues: "Moreover, genuine pioneering calls for and requires considerable sacrifices to be made by the settler; only the strong incentive to make the land produce as soon as possible will stimulate the settler to the utmost. No one would wish for a return

partly by loans from the Export-Import Bank and AID and partly by the Peruvian Government, this 50-mile ribbon, built by a Peruvian construction firm, will open for development an area estimated at 237,000 acres capable of being developed for crops, cattle, or timber. The road to Tocache, built by the Ministry of Public Works, will eventually continue north from Tocache until it connects with the Juanjuí-Tarapoto road leading to the Northern Trans-Andean (Olmos-Yurimaguas) Highway.

Thus, when the aforementioned highway system is completed, the entire Central Huallaga Valley will have road access to the Pan American Highway and the Pacific Coast. In anticipation of this development, a United Nations Special Fund project, administered by the Food and Agriculture Organization (FAO) and the Peruvian National Office of Agrarian Reform (ONRA) at a cost of U.S. $3.5 million, is now studying the natural, economic, and human resources of the 8,645,000-acre Central Huallaga, Imaza, and Nieva basins. With headquarters in Tarapoto, and a staff of international and Peruvian specialists, this Huallaga Project 1966–70 "will survey the river basins, prepare plans for overall rural development and, finally, assist the Peruvian Government to carry out specific projects for use of the regions' natural resources."[16]

On the Oriente sector of the Central Trans-Andean Highway (Lima to Pucallpa), noted earlier, a rebuilding and rerouting program began in 1962 with the arrival of a shipload of construction equipment in Pucallpa by way of the Amazon and Ucayali rivers. The former muddy, rutted road of the rainy season is now the Peruvian East's only two-lane *paved* highway, surfaced with a double bituminous treatment. From Pucallpa to Aguaytía, vehicles can speed year round on this "superhighway" through lowland jungle, over new and rehabilitated bridges. It has long been planned to push this road eastward from Pucallpa to the border with Brazil,

---

to the unplanned, unaided colonization efforts of earlier years where total failure and a high toll of human suffering, disease and misery was exacted by the remorseless conditions of living in the jungle, but if La Morada is to be in any way a pilot scheme whose formula for success is to be repeated elsewhere, every effort should be made to limit credit to initial periods and essential establishment costs, and thereafter for it to be loaned in a 'pump priming' way to stimulate further agricultural expansion. Certainly, clearing does not need to be financed, for young fit colonists can each clear one hectare in 20–30 days; yet this is regularly provided for in credit loans."

16. *Peruvian Times*, March 25, 1966, p. 10.

a nation rushing construction of its own Trans-Amazon Highway which will reach Cruzeiro do Sul and the Peruvian frontier. The speed with which the Brazilians are going forward with the construction of their own national highway should make the Peruvians anxious to complete as quickly as possible their own road eastward from Pucallpa to the frontier with Brazil.

In mid-1964, construction was completed on the first highway into the 40,000-square-mile wilderness between the Apurímac and Urubamba rivers in south central Peru. This single lane dirt road, a 30-mile extension of the highway from Huanta, winds its way over two passes (13,288 feet and 12,303 feet) before descending to the Apurímac River at the small settlement of San Francisco de Apurímac (2,800 feet). It was also founded in 1964, at the edge of the Vilcabamba jungle region, a rugged range of forest-covered mountain in which the first traverse was recorded only in 1963 by four members of the Vilcabamba Expedition of the National Geographic Society and the New York Zoological Society. Now yielding to a gradual influx of population (noted previously), the Peruvian Government is planning to entice settlers even more by completing a bridge over the Apurímac and continuing the road in both directions on the eastern bank of the Apurímac to the Mapitunuari and Quimpiri rivers. Feasibility studies have been funded for a road in the Perené-Satipo zone and the lower reaches of the Apurímac, where the river takes the names Ene and Tambo, and for a road northward to Puerto Pachitea, all part of the projected Marginal Forest Highway which will eventually cross this area to the Urubamba and Madre de Dios valleys, to Puerto Maldonado and into Bolivia.

In southeastern Peru new settlement is slowly increasing and consumer goods are flowing by truck rather than solely by airplane, this a result of the 150-mile road opened in 1965 from Quincemil to Puerto Maldonado, a town of 10,000, long oriented to Brazil and Bolivia. This is an area made even more accessible by the 504-foot, single-span suspension bridge over the Inambari River; it was officially inaugurated by the president in 1966. Serranos on road construction crews or under contract to local *hacendados* have remained in the area, now growing bananas, yuca, tea, coffee, corn, rice, and citrus on their small farms (*chacras*). Near Puerto Maldonado an internationally financed, still embryonic, colonization project, under the leadership of a jungle physician, a native of

Spain, is contracting the colonist by providing him transportation expenses, food, and shelter until he is established on his 37 acres; grain storage tanks, a rice-drying plant, power plant, and sawmill have been installed. Inhabitants of the area are hopeful that a road will eventually bore northward from Puerto Maldonado to Iñapari—at the rubber-rich junction of the territories of Peru, Brazil, and Bolivia—and connect with the planned transcontinental highway through the Brazilian state of Acre.

With Peru's tremendous outlay of funds and energy for this selvatic road network, and after observing the enthusiasm of a Belaúnde Terry, one hesitates even to whisper, "But is it worth it?" Could not this expenditure be steered to more economical development projects in the populated areas? Settlement in the low selva is concentrated, and will continue to be, on the alluvial riverine soils where products can be easily boated, even long distances, to roadheads; cultivation of other lands is not profitable for the small farmer who cannot put to use the costly suggestions of optimistic planners to make his land produce. And not until more pasture research has been completed can the long-run possibilities of ranching be reasonably predicted.

We conclude with Wesche that "Not only the massive immigration to the montaña but also part of the outmigration from the area attests to the vigorous role which the montaña frontier already plays in the country's economic development. Past migration response to new settlement opportunities, the large number of visitors in search of new land which one encounters throughout the western montaña, and the distinct trend toward permanent settlement leave no doubt that the momentum of montaña development will increase as the government commits greater resources to the provision of roads, medical and education facilities, extension and credit services, while promoting an agrarian reform which favors the small-scale owner. One of the most striking features of future montaña development will be the massive involvement of highland Indians for whom the montaña offers a brighter future for upward mobility than is available to them in urban centers."[17]

OVERVIEW

To the elite, work on the Carretera Marginal during President Fernando Belaúnde Terry's regime was merely a needless drain on

17. Rolf Wesche, "Recent Migration to the Peruvian Montaña," p. 265.

the nation's treasury; it did show, however, that there was a promising frontier in the East. The revolutionary government that succeeded Belaúnde Terry, less dependent on elite support than most of its predecessors, vigorously supports continuing construction of this Marginal Forest Highway, for it is anxious to develop the untamed montaña frontier. Increased agricultural production in the montaña means expansion of the internal market, an important consideration in this era of exacerbating economic nationalism. The dramatic growth of Peru's population—3.2 per cent per year—is another reason why the military government seeks the effective incorporation into the nation of this vast empty quarter. And one must not overlook the strategic importance in countering the westward expansion of the Brazilian colossus and the expansionist aims of Ecuador.

The most promising alternative to excessive urbanization is a major expansion of the agricultural sector of the economy, and this would be of greatest benefit to the masses of rural Indians. The rural Indian, in general unprepared to function effectively in the urban world, is willing to continue farming if given economic incentives and assurance of modest improvements in his level of living. And free land—in abundance—is available; its valorization requires only the most basic infrastructure and services. In the past, the highland Indians have come to the eastern lowlands largely as seasonal laborers rather than as permanent settlers, and have preferred locations close to their areas of origin to permit continuing contact. Indian settlers are now distributed throughout the accessible sectors of the eastern valleys and piedmont alluvial plain.

Montaña colonization has in general proceeded in narrow bands along a few existing penetration roads and their trail, river, and feeder road extensions. But powerful individuals acquire the frontage sectors in vast tracts along these transportation arteries, effectively blocking access to the interior. Mestizos and whites with capital, and often with government backing, monopolize choice land in the more active, promising, and better serviced colonization zones of the central and northern montaña; the Indians, without resources and skills, come as seasonal or long-term laborers on the large landholdings, rather than penetrating the unoccupied terrain more remote and less attractive. Furthermore, the Indians of the central and northern sierra migrate along the available roads to the major coastal cities and plantation areas and to the principal sierran mining sectors rather than to the tropical lowlands to the east. The southern Peruvian montaña has poor quality penetration roads, inadequate access to markets, and almost complete absence of services. Coastal areas and mining centers are remote, and few whites and mestizos, and even fewer large entrepreneurs, have been attracted to this southern montaña. However, during the 1960s the Indians of the densely populated sierran zone, possessing nothing but their labor and with limited economic aspirations, have poured down the eastern slopes of the Andes. They have established homogeneous Indian settlements which provide the stability and feeling of security so characteristic of the immemorial communities of the Sierra. Since Indian recipients of government land have proved to be more stable settlers than their mestizo counterparts, it is almost certain that continued access to suitable land and availability of government assistance and adequate services would assure massive Indian participation in montaña development.

Infrastructure investments in the montaña can yield maximum returns under a master plan that coordinates land, river, and air transportation facilities and orderly land settlement. Economic opportunity is a sufficient trigger for inducing immigration and settlement in the first place, but the availability of basic services determines the degree of settlement stability and the intensive management of land. The current socioeconomic reforms of the "revolutionary" government, carried out in existing areas of settlement along the coast and in the sierra, represent temporary and partial solutions to the problem of demographic pressure on the resource base, solutions unable to arrest a deterioration of living conditions on a national scale that could create explosive revolutionary potential. Regional autonomy in eastern Peru should be envisaged by those with capital—both government and private—to invest. Intraregional transportation facilities will help facilitate the establishment of regional manufacturing centers with their related urban employment alternatives and full range of services.

Thus, the country has a highly developed coastal zone, a relatively underdeveloped sierran section with a dense Indian population, and a dynamic, rapidly developing montaña that includes more than half of the country. If a better balance between man and his resource base can be achieved by valorizing this great eastern sector of the nation, the future of Peru will be more stable than its past.

References: Peru

Arthur D. Little, Inc. "Plan Peru-Via: A Preliminary Evaluation of the Peru-Via Area of Peru, with a Proposed Plan for Approaching the Development of Its Resources." In *A Program for the Industrial and Regional Development of Peru*, pp. 57–116 (1960).

Belaúnde Terry, Fernando. *La carretera marginal de la selva*. Lima, 1964.

———. *Peru's Own Conquest*. Lima: American Studies Press S.A., 1965.

Cavero-Egúsquiza y Saavedra, Ricardo. *La Amazonia peruana*. Lima: Imprenta Torres Aguirre, 1941.

Comité Interamericano de Desarrollo Agrícola. *Tenencia de la tierra y desarrollo socio-económico del sector agrícola: Perú*. Washington: Pan American Union, 1965.

Coriat, Juan E. *El hombre del Amazonas y ensayo monográfico de Loreto*. 2d ed. Lima: Librería Coriat-Imprenta, 1943.

Coutu, Arthur J., and King, Richard A. *The Agricultural Development of Peru*. Praeger Special Studies in International Economics and Development. New York: Frederick A. Praeger, 1969.

Crist, Raymond E. "Conceptos generales sobre la colonización en la Montaña peruana." *Estudios de Población Desarrollo* 3, no. 3 (Marzo 1969):1–16.

Delboy, Emilio. *Colonización y caminos en la selva: La Empresa LeTourneau*. Lima: D. Miranda, 1954.

———. "Memorandum sobre la selva del Perú." *Boletin de la Sociedad Geográfica de Lima* 69 (primer y segundo trimestre, 1952):3–52.

Denevan, William M. "The Carretera Marginal de la Selva and the Central Huallaga Region of Peru." *Geographical Review* 56, no. 3 (July 1966):440–43.

"El desarrollo de regiones desconocidas." *Visión* 32, no. 8 (March 31, 1967):20–24.

Dobyns, Henry F., and Vázquez, Mario C., eds. *Migración e integración en el Perú*. Monografías andinas, no. 2. Lima: Editorial Estudios Andinos, 1963.

Drewes, Wolfram U. *The Economic Development of the Western Montaña of Central Peru Related to Transportation*. Lima: Peruvian Times, 1958.

Eidt, Robert C. "Economic Features of Land Opening in the Peruvian Montaña." *Professional Geographer* 18, no. 3 (May 1966):146–50.

———. "Pioneer Settlement in Eastern Peru." *Annals of the Association of American Geographers* 52, no. 3 (September 1962):255–78.

Figueroa, Pedro T. *Lima-Cerro, Huánuco-Pucallpa, la mejor via troncal del Pacífico al Amazonas*. Lima: Sanmarti y Cía., 1934.

Ford, Thomas R. *Man and Land in Peru*. Gainesville: University of Florida Press, 1952.

Fry, Carlos. *La gran región de los bosques; o, Ríos peruanos navegables: Urubamba, Ucayali, Amazonas, Pachitea y Palcazu. Diario de viajes y exploraciones por Carlos Fry en 1886, 1887 y 1888*. Lima: Imprenta de B. Gil, 1889.

Girard, Rafael. *Indios selváticos de la Amazonia peruana*. México, D.F.: Libro Max Editores, 1958.

Hall, Clarence W. *Two Thousand Tongues to Go*. Lima: Pacific Press, S.A., 1958.

Holmberg, Allan R. "Changing Community Attitudes and Values in Peru: A Case Study in Guided Change." In *Social Change in Latin America Today: Its Implications for United States Policy*. New York: Harper and Brothers, for the Council on Foreign Relations, 1960.

Kuczynski-Godard, Maxime H. *La vida en la Amazonia peruana*. Lima: Librería Internacional del Perú, S.A., 1944.

Lathrap, Donald W. "The Cultural Sequence at Yarinacocha, Eastern Peru." *American Antiquity* 23, no. 4 (April 1958):379–88.

Maass, Alfredo, *Entwicklung und Perspektiven der wirtschaftlichen Erschliessung des tropischen Waldlandes von Peru, unter besonderer Berücksichtigung der verkehrs geographischen Problematik.* Tübingen: Universität Tübingen, 1969.

McBride, George McCutchen, and McBride, Merle A. "Peruvian Avenues of Penetration into Amazonia." *Geographical Review* 34, no. 1 (January 1944):1–35.

Nuñez del Prado C., Oscar. *Sicuani: un pueblo grande, reacción social para la colonización de Maldonado.* Lima: Ministerio de Trabajo y Asuntos Indígenas, 1962.

Peru. Ministerio de Fomento. *Inauguración de la carretera Lima-Huánuco-Pucallpa.* Boletín Extraordinario. Lima, 1943.

Peruvian Colonization. Brochure printed and distributed by LeTourneau del Perú, Inc., Longview, Texas.

Peruvian Times (Lima). 1950–73.

Pinedo del Aguila, Víctor M. "Formaciones humanas de la selva amazónica peruana." *Boletín de la Sociedad Geográfica de Lima* 69 (tercero y cuarto trimestre, 1952):62–78.

———. "La hilea amazónica peruana." *Boletín de la Sociedad Geográfica de Lima* 65 (primer y segundo trimestre, 1948):14–24.

Robinson, David A. *Peru in Four Dimensions.* Lima: American Studies Press S.A., 1964.

Steward, Julian H., and Métraux, Alfred. "Tribes of the Peruvian and Ecuadorian Montaña." *Handbook of South American Indians*, Bureau of American Ethnology Bulletins, no. 143. 6 vols. (Washington, 1948), 3:535–656.

Stewart, Norman R. "Migration and Settlement in the Peruvian Montaña: The Apurímac Valley." *Geographical Review* 55, no. 2 (April 1965):143–57.

Tanner, Louise Bentley. *The Jungle Indians of Peru and the Work of the Summer Institute of Linguistics.* Lima: Pacific Press, S.A., 1956.

Vázquez, Jesús María, O.P. *Pucallpa: estudio socio-religioso de una ciudad del Perú.* Madrid: Editorial O.P.E., 1962.

Villarejo, Avencio. *Así es la selva; geografía general de la selva baja.* Lima: Compañía de Impresiones y Publicidad, 1943.

———. *La selva y el hombre, estudio antropocosmológico del aborigen amazónico.* Lima: Editorial Ausonia, S.A., 1959.

Watson Cisneros, Eduardo. *Comercio y tendencias del mercado en los productos de la región de la selva peruana.* Lima: Universidad Agraria, 1964.

Watters, R. F. "Shifting Cultivation in Peru." F.A.O. Report, 1965. Typescript.

Wesche, Rolf. "Recent Migration to the Peruvian Montaña." *Cahiers de Géographie de Québec*, Quinzième Année, no. 35 (Septembre 1971), pp. 251–65.

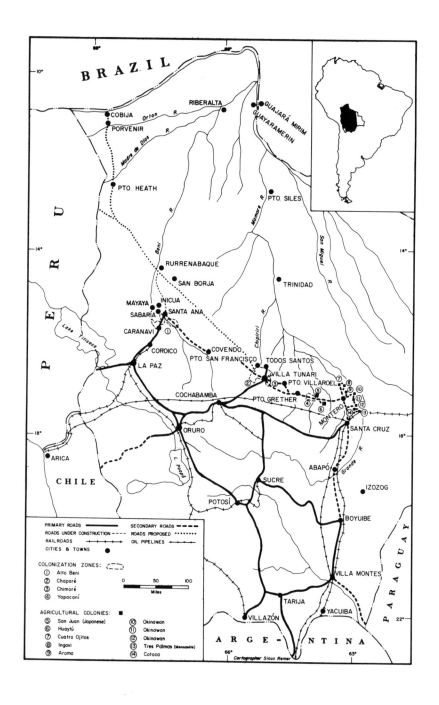

PRIMARY ROADS ━━━━━━ SECONDARY ROADS ━ ━ ━
ROADS UNDER CONSTRUCTION ━ ━ ━ ━ ROADS PROPOSED ⋯⋯⋯⋯
RAILROADS ┼┼┼┼┼┼ OIL PIPELINES ┼━┼━┼
CITIES & TOWNS ●

COLONIZATION ZONES: ⌇⌇⌇
① Alto Beni
② Chaparé
③ Chimoré
④ Yapacaní

0   50   100
Miles

AGRICULTURAL COLONIES: ■
⑤ San Juan (Japanese)   ⑩ Okinawan
⑥ Huaytú   ⑪ Okinawan
⑦ Cuatro Ojitos   ⑫ Okinawan
⑧ Ingavi   ⑬ Tres Palmas (Mennonite)
⑨ Aroma   ⑭ Cotoca

Cartographer Sioux Remer

6. Bolivia

For the Indians of the Bolivian Altiplano, the old order changes, but its passing should not be mourned; for "all that local flavor covered up great human misery; the day of the integration of the Andean Indians into modern life will remain one of the great dates in the history of American nations." The quotation is from Jean Albert Vellard,[1] who has degrees in both medicine and anthropology, and who has spent most of the past quarter century in field investigations in Andean America. The Indian is sympathetically pictured against the backdrop of snow-capped mountains of multicolored metamorphic rocks, granites, and sandstones; of dark blue skies where huge cumulus clouds float; and of bleak, windswept foothills and inhospitable salt flats. To be sure, the Indian for centuries thought of his high, cold homeland as the center of the world, but a world where "sun, lakes, mountains, and winds, all are forces which ceaselessly play man false, the influence of which must, if one is to live at peace, be placated by magic rites."[2]

By the end of the nineteenth century, the Indian had begun to realize that his fellow men, particularly the governing clique, could be a sinister force that must be countered, and without benefit of magic. In 1899, when the Indians were forced to become "revolutionaries" under General Pando and definitively put the *mestizo* in power, they took home to their villages a vision of the role they might someday play. In 1945, when the first government of the reform party, Movimiento Nacionalista Revolucionario (MNR), was in power, Villarroel decreed the abolition of forced, unpaid labor on the great estates and in the town houses of absentee landowners. The MNR Revolution of 1952 was not just another in the long

1. *Civilisations des Andes: évolution des populations du haut-plateau bolivien*, p. 262.
2. Ibid., p. 9.

series of "palace" revolutions, for at that time more power than ever before passed into the hands of the Indian masses. Shortly thereafter, agrarian reforms were initiated, the three leading tin-mining companies were nationalized, and the army was virtually disbanded, to be replaced at least in the early years by peasants' and miners' militias.

The towering Cordillera Real northeast of La Paz has for centuries been a mighty barrier to migration from the Altiplano to the warm foothills and plains of the Oriente. (The road from La Paz to the Yungas climbs to a pass more than 15,000 feet high and drops 14,000 feet to the Beni lowlands within a distance of 50 miles.) Settlers have been attracted to the valleys of the Yungas, the intermediate belt between the high Cordillera and the great plains to the east, first by the lure of gold, rubber, and cinchona, then by the possibility of producing coca, coffee, and sugar. For the new government agrarian reform was a sine qua non in the development of the nation. From August 1953 to December 1959, no fewer than 46,857 titles to land, amounting to 1,535,000 acres, were granted to 36,603 heads of families. Beginning in July 1960, the National Council of Agrarian Reform began to award 20,000 additional land titles and in that same month distributed 142,000 acres in plots averaging 25 to 30 acres. In 1962 a high of 1,880 properties were expropriated (50,227 titles and 1,320,000 acres granted), decreasing to 202 in 1965 (15,600 titles and 306,500 acres granted).[3]

SANTA CRUZ

The Santa Cruz area was regarded as the most likely sector in which to achieve a rapid increase in the domestic production of foodstuffs and other agricultural raw materials, for here thousands of acres of fertile and cultivable land lying idle constituted a *Lebensraum* of heroic proportions. Specifically, the broad piedmont alluvial plain, paralleling the eastern range of the Andes, could support hundreds of thousands of people in a salubrious area almost entirely free of mosquitoes. By 1962, the various centers of colonization under the government agency Acción Andina, military authorities, or private persons amounted to more than 2,500 families in the Santa Cruz area. In addition, some 2,000 families had

3. Alexander T. Edelmann, "Colonization in Bolivia: Progress and Prospects," pp. 39–41.

reached the Chaparé sector, by using the new "jeepable" road from the Cochabamba Valley.

Santa Cruz de la Sierra is often nicknamed Santa Cruz de la Tierra, with good reason: the town is famous for its violent wind and sand storms during the *surazos* (storms from the south) of the dry season. With the sun burning down from the light blue, cloud-less sky, the wind shrieks and whistles along the narrow, sandy, un-paved streets, lifting dust and sand into the air, until the whole town is shrouded in a pall of dust and haze, like the *calina* of the Spanish summer. Sand dunes are piled deep on the old brick side-walks that line the streets, sheltered from the rains of the wet season by the projecting second stories or roofs of the houses. After a wind-storm of several days' duration, one hears everywhere the sound of shovels scraping on sidewalks, as in the middle latitudes after a snow storm. But this sand and dust are by no means clean, for there is no sewerage in Santa Cruz; drains empty freely into the street.

Santa Cruz de la Sierra was originally located in the Andean foothills and early supplied the mountain towns of Charcas (now Sucre) and Potosí with sugar, rice, preserved fruits, and cotton thread. Founded in 1561 by an eighty-man expedition from Asun-ción under the leadership of the Spanish explorer Ñuflo de Chaves,[4] the city was moved between 1601 and 1604 to its present site 150 miles westward, 20 miles from the foot of the Andes. The town be-came an outpost of the west, its chief function being to supply the adjacent highlands with tropical produce, particularly cane sugar.

The Spaniards subjugated the indigenous population, organizing the people into settlements for cattle ranching or for the production of sugar or cotton. It was not a frontier zone, in the sense of a frontier zone of continuous pioneering activity such as was pushed across the United States. Rather, the Spaniards created small cul-tural and economic islands in a vast wilderness where nomadic hunting and some slash-and-burn agriculture were the principal activities of a sparse population. The town of Santa Cruz, the com-mercial center and capital of a large province within the Charcas Audiencia, was for centuries an outpost of the west. Bolivia con-tinued to be practically self-sufficient in foodstuffs. The plains of Santa Cruz for years filled the domestic demand for sugar and rice

---

4. Hernando Sanabria Fernández, *Ñuflo de Chaves: el caballero andante de la selva*, p. 263.

and even exported those items to southern Peru and northern Argentina.

The building of railroads at the end of the nineteenth century revolutionized the economy of Andean Bolivia, for the export of minerals from the highlands facilitated the importing of foreign agricultural products of higher quality and lower price than domestic produce. Hence, it was not profitable to extend the railroads into the eastern lowlands. Santa Cruz could only suffer from economic stagnation, for it ceased to be an outpost of the west. Yet it was not incorporated into any other system; it lived on in the heart of the continent in a state of splendid isolation but also in a state of suspended animation.

By 1930, Santa Cruz was the center of a world apart; there was air service to Cochabamba and Puerto Suárez, oxcart trails to the east, north, and south, and a mule trail to Cochabamba—a two-week trip! The trails from Santa Cruz to Puerto Suárez, Embarcación, Cochabamba, and Montero were improved enough during the 1930s to permit the movement of cars and trucks during the dry season, but the government feared, perhaps with reason, that the secessionist tendencies of Santa Cruz would be encouraged if roads or railroads were to connect it with Brazil and Argentina. Yet, because of lack of funds, the proposed government railway from Cochabamba to Santa Cruz was not constructed. Very little work was done even on the construction of the highway between these points. At the same time, Bolivia was plagued by inflation, and, in order to keep down the cost of living, imported foodstuffs were given preferential treatment while prices to domestic producers were set at unrealistically low levels. Thus, foreign producers were in reality being subsidized while the Bolivian farmers were discriminated against—all in the name of benefiting the Bolivian consumer. The powerful mining companies continued to oppose national self-sufficiency in agricultural production; such development would not only reduce the nation's dependence on the earnings of mineral exports, but would also provide increased opportunities of alternative employment for the low-paid mine workers. Further, the nation was in many respects "Balkanized." Santa Cruz, for instance, imposed local taxes of 2 to 5 per cent on most goods leaving or entering the area. Thus, the isolation and stagnation of the Bolivian Oriente were due as much to man-made economic barriers as to physical remoteness or inaccessibility.

In spite of such conditions, Santa Cruz Department increased in population from 200,000 in 1900 to 286,000 in 1950,[5] to some 450,000 in 1972, whereas the town grew seven-fold in the same period, from 18,000 to 43,000[6] to over 120,000. The 1900–1950 population increase was largely the result of the growth of the local population, not immigration. Thereafter, immigration constituted a significant element in the increase.

The dominant socioeconomic structure was the *finca*, or great landed estate, many of which had survived from colonial days. Very few of these great estates had ever been surveyed; indeed, most landholders had no legal titles to their properties, which were worked by peasants of three types: *inquilinos* (sharecroppers), *jornaleros* (day workers), and *tolerados* (squatters). Free land was available for the taking, but it was safer to live near the big house of the great landlord, for wild Indians sometimes roved the forest. Further, the fincas were not too remote from markets, which could be reached over a narrow oxcart trail, often impassable in the rainy season. Squatters cleared land on the more inaccessible parts of the great estates, and grew rice, sugar, bananas, and yuca, on a subsistence basis; they paid no rent. They could work as day laborers at harvest season, but they were also subject to having their clearings appropriated by the landowner, or *finquero*, at his pleasure.

Rice, maize, yuca, and cooking bananas were the basic items of the subsistence diet, grown on small plots and large, for the use of owner and worker alike. Small quantities of coffee, coca, citrus fruits, peanuts, and vegetables were also grown. Cattle were grazed on natural grasslands and were driven to local markets to be used as fresh meat or to be made into jerked beef. The principal cash crop was sugarcane; small amounts of brown sugar were made for use on the finca or for sale in Santa Cruz, but by far the larger part was made into the much more valuable and easily transported alcohol. During World War II, the Bolivian Development Corporation had, with United States aid, pushed such projects as a large sugar mill, intensification of land use, mechanization of rice-growing, cultivation of artificial pastures, upgrading of livestock. But only during the past decade have really significant changes taken place.

5. Bolivia, Ministerio de Hacienda, Dirección General de Estadística, *Boletín estadístico 1964*, no. 90, p. 60.
6. J. Valerie Fifer, "Bolivia's Pioneer Fringe," p. 17.

After the Revolution of 1952, the peasants precariously living on the tiny plots—the *minifundia*—in the exhausted lands of the over-populated highlands, as well as the miners left jobless as a result of the decline in the tin mining industry, were encouraged to migrate to Santa Cruz, to the east. And technical assistance has been made increasingly available by both the United Nations and the United States. By 1954, high-yielding Cuban yellow corn was planted almost universally near Santa Cruz, and high-yielding strains of rice and sugarcane were distributed. Another service distributes for sale, at or below cost, such items as seeds, fertilizers, insecticides, tools, and seed bulls.

Indeed, a great deal of technical assistance has been necessary to aid in the general migration from the Altiplano and valleys of highland Bolivia to the Santa Cruz area—an altitudinal descent from between 8,000 and 14,000 feet above sea level to 1,000 feet. Further, the climate changes from cold to tropical and the subsistence economy is exchanged for one in which emphasis is placed on market-oriented agriculture. The Quechua and Aymara culture of the highlands is replaced by one in which the Spanish language is dominant.

The agricultural status quo is also being altered as a result of immigration. Settlements are made up of both Bolivians and foreigners: soldiers mustered out of service, former mine workers from Potosí and Oruro, and Quechua peasants who once migrated to the sugar plantations of northern Argentina as harvest laborers. Notwithstanding, a major obstacle to lowland colonization has reportedly been the resistance of highland Indian women to migration. Yet, South Italians, Mennonites of Volga-German and Dutch-German stock, Japanese, and Okinawans, from their respective colonies, mingle in the shops and markets with both highland and lowland Indians and mestizos.

The United States provided the surveys, construction work, and financing of the Santa Cruz–Cochabamba highway, officially opened in 1954 and now a significant link in the communication network of Bolivia; its primary purpose was to tie Santa Cruz firmly to the national economy. Leaving Cochabamba, this paved road goes through a stern, even melancholy country, with high rugged mountains on either side, destitute of trees, yet here and there adorned with tiny grain fields, plastered precariously on steep, forbidding slopes. Deep down in the valleys is seen the verdant line where the

irrigating stream makes it possible for men to gain the upper hand
in their struggle against the steep, rocky desert. Almost halfway between Cochabamba and Santa Cruz, along a sector called La Siberia, resembling some of the wilder landscapes on Japanese
screens, ascending, warm, moisture-laden air currents from the east,
pushed across the mountain crest, yield enough precipitation to
support a dense stand of cloud forest for a mile or more downslope
on the leeward side. Here lumbering is being carried on. Beyond
the desert valley of Matorral, at kilometer 314 out of Cochabamba,
one enters a valley in which there are many recent settlers who raise
corn on new clearings in the forest. The town of Valle Grande lies
off to the right.

Except for the timber resources of La Siberia and the recent settlements near Valle Grande, the Cochabamba–Santa Cruz highway
straddles a poor, almost deserted section. To be sure, truckloads of
cattle for slaughter, sugar, lumber, and rice reach the highlands
over this highway, but it is, nevertheless, in many respects like a
road connecting two oases that does not now have, nor ever will
have, feeder roads to it.

Petroleum.—In the past twenty years the Bolivian Gulf Oil Company, a wholly owned subsidiary of Gulf Oil Company, has invested
more than $50 million in explorations in its concession area within
a radius of 550 miles of Santa Cruz. By the end of 1964, 55 of 101
wells drilled had proved productive, and production continues to
rise.[7] Gulf was given confidence in its explorations by concessions of
the Bolivian government and by the fact that oil investments of
United States companies abroad are insured against foreign con-
fiscatory legislation by what amounts to almost total reimburse-
ment. Thus, Gulf has built a 360-mile, 12-inch pipeline from Santa
Cruz to Sica Sica, designed to carry 50,000 barrels a day. From Sica
Sica to Arica, oil flows through the 210-mile pipeline of the YPFB
(Yacimientos Petrolíferos Fiscales Bolivianos). Initial shipments of
30,000 b/d of crude from the Caranda field were made, a gas pipeline to the Argentine border was completed, and refining capacity
increased.

However, in spite of the original concessions, the Bolivian government expropriated the Gulf Company on October 17, 1969, charg-

7. Petroleum production increased from 967,400 cubic meters in 1966 to
2,382,800 cubic meters in 1968 (*Europa Yearbook 1970*, 2:106).

ing that the company was not exploiting its holdings in the national interest.

Cotton.—Imports of cotton, mostly from Peru and the United States, necessary to supply the needs of an expanding cotton textile industry, have for years consumed a great deal of badly needed Bolivian exchange. The government has pushed a campaign of increasing cotton production, with the result that cotton acreage in the Santa Cruz area more than doubled from 1964 to 1966—from 3,500 acres to 8,250. With more cotton produced domestically for Bolivia's textile mills—some 6,000 bales were ginned in 1965—the government hopes to reduce the smuggling into the country of finished textiles, particularly from Brazil. The government's premise is that, as customs revenues increase, the market for domestic textiles will be stimulated.

Sugar.—The report of Chardón and Leigh is a most perceptive and prophetic work on the development of the sugar industry in the Department of Santa Cruz.[8] They concluded that a coordinated program of action could make the sugar industry, already established in the Santa Cruz area, capable of supplying the demand of the entire nation; emphasis should be placed on the production of rice, citrus, cattle, vegetable oils, coffee, and cacao. Such coordinated development of agriculture and animal husbandry envisages an intranational immigration of perhaps 100,000 families, particularly from the overcrowded Altiplano and intermontane valleys. It is postulated that this immigration would use the routes to the Alto Beni and to Santa Cruz.

Argentine-Bolivian Railway.—Another factor in the expansion of opportunities in the Santa Cruz sector is the construction of the railroad from Argentina. Built over a period of twenty years with Argentine money (an estimated $25 million) and Argentine experience, it was inaugurated in 1957, but formally declared open only in 1966. Bolivia is using oil to pay for its construction, a product badly needed in Argentina. It is hoped during the next few years to continue the track as far as Ichilo, a port on the Yapacaní River, which flows into the Mamoré and ultimately into the Amazon. High hopes have been placed on this railway, tapping as it does an area rich in choice hardwoods and fertile alluvial soils. The construction

8. Carlos E. Chardón and Stephen Leigh, *Desarrollo de la industria azucarera en el Departamento de Santa Cruz: informe (con una introducción sobre sus proyecciones en el planeamiento de la economía nacional).*

of this railway is another significant step forward in opening up eastern Bolivia to the forces of modernity, another step in making it possible for the inhabitants there to think in terms of a wider national as well as international market.

River transport.—The roads that have been built eastward from La Paz and Cochabamba will ultimately connect with river ports on the headwaters of the Beni and Mamoré rivers. Modern barges and tow boats, as well as small dugout canoes powered by outboard motors, will overcome that great barrier, space, that has thus far prevented this vast sector from becoming the nationally integrated economic region that it would seem destined by nature to become. It is perhaps too early to talk in terms of the Beni and Mamoré rivers playing the role in the evolution of Bolivia that the Mississippi and Missouri rivers did a century ago for the development of the Midwest of the United States; however, it is possible to envision greater economic growth, once transportation is provided for settlers who grow more crops and who have the advantages of modern education and public health measures.

Brazilian-Bolivian Railway.—The Brazilian railroad from Santos on the Atlantic to the frontier with Bolivia in Corumbá was gradually extended some 300 miles through the forests of eastern Bolivia to reach Santa Cruz; the service is reputed to be very poor, with breakdowns and derailments common. At the present time, the Corumbá–Santa Cruz line supports much small-time smuggling, to judge from the Brazilian products available in the stores in Santa Cruz. However, this road is certainly destined to play a very important role in opening up this vast area to settlement.

Colonization and Settlement in the Santa Cruz Area

With 93 per cent of Bolivia's population concentrated in 41 per cent of the national territory, the 1952 Social Revolution emphasized agrarian reform as a primary objective to relieve population pressure on the Altiplano and western mountain slopes, to advance political unity, and to check unemployment and underemployment in the nationalized tin-mining industry. And to settle the virgin eastern lands, Bolivia has fostered the development of foreign colonies—Mennonite, Japanese, Okinawan—in the Santa Cruz area as models for the Bolivian farmers who have been resettled from the overpopulated highlands into the forested vastness of eastern Bolivia.

The Corporación Boliviana de Fomento (CBF), using the manpower of the Bolivian army, prepared the Yapacaní–Puerto Grether area to the west of the town of Santa Cruz for a new colonization project in 1958 by widening the path between the two sites. The soldiers cleared the forest, planted a belt, twenty yards wide, of rice, corn, yuca, and plantains in the fertile soils of alluvial silt along the fifteen-mile road, and constructed temporary houses. Crops and houses were soon requisitioned by sporadically arriving colonizers. The improvement of the road in 1961, providing four-hour marketing access to the city of Santa Cruz, brought increased spontaneous colonization, mainly from the Departments of Cochabamba, Potosí, and Santa Cruz, by settlers receiving no promise of assistance on their individual 75-acre plots. Many were "wait-and-see" settlers, preceding their wives by as much as two years. The army, however, managed to provide medical care, mosquito nets, tools, a teacher, and assistance in house construction. Even more important to their survival, the colonizers, until realizing an existence from their lands, worked—and many still do so—as day laborers in the nearby Japanese colony of San Juan during harvesting periods.

Approximately 1,100 families on 83,000 acres now are included in the Yapacaní zone, in 1961 made a part of the sponsored CBF / BID (Banco Interamericano de Desarrollo) colonization program.

Cattle raising on these rapidly leached soils—the area has over 100 inches average annual rainfall—is an important aspect of the settlement program. Cultivating a higher average of fifteen acres, principally rice (nine acres) and corn (five acres), and profiting by easy, though high cost, truck access to the Santa Cruz market, the Yapacaní settler surpasses in annual income his counterpart in the spontaneous zones of Chaparé and Caranavi.[9] Many colonizers of the Yapacaní also benefit from their banana crop, which is now selling in Santa Cruz but may reach profitable Argentina export markets.

Directed colonization, in the more immediate vicinity of the de-

9. The Santa Cruz area also features, besides an estimated 3,500 squatter families scattered along the roads opened the last ten years, the spontaneous colonies of Ingavi (established in 1963, with a 1965 population of 420 families on 30,000 acres), San Luis Angostura (established in 1953, with a 1965 population of 877 families on 35,000 acres), and Bañado Grande (established in 1961, with a 1965 population of 266 families on 6,700 acres). Francisco Sánchez V. and Kelso L. Wessel, "Resumen de tres zonas de colonización y comparación de la agricultura del Oriente con el Altiplano," p. 56.

partmental capital, was initiated in 1955 near Cotoca by the United Nations Andean Mission (Misión Andina) and the Organización Internacional de Trabajadores (OIT). In this pilot project, in a sandy-soil, limited-rainfall area where forest gives way to grassland, eighteen miles east of Santa Cruz, thirty-two Quechua-speaking colonists arrived in July; some were selected from the village of Calcha (Department of Potosí) with previous seasonal migratory experience on the sugar plantations of northern Argentina, others from Potosí were miners with farming experience. All were over eighteen in age, certified in good health and of good behavior, and were promised land, homes ready for occupancy, seed, and medical-educational-technical assistance.

And, upon arrival, the colonists encountered just that—promises, quite empty; the most elementary of precolonization efforts, delineation of the settlement area, had not even been completed. They settled in the town of Cotoca, sowed lands lent by the local government, and worked for the project as jornaleros to make a reality of those unfulfilled precolonization promises.[10] Soon delimited, the colonization zone was divided into two parts, La Enconada and El Campanario, each with a communal center. It was here, rather than on a twenty-five-acre lot, that the early colonists erected brick and tile dwellings.

Resources now poured into this showcase of colonization projects: a large administrative staff (all Bolivians except the director, a member of OIT); formation of a cooperative with voluntary participation; schools, shops, health posts; tractors and trucks; a one-year supply of food free; an agronomy engineer, a veterinarian, a doctor, a home economics teacher, a social worker, an instructor in carpentry. Not all was free, however, for one-half of the costs of settlement had to be repaid within five years. This burden, made even less bearable by low soil fertility and the early 1963 withdrawal of almost all aid (totaling over half a million dollars since 1955), disheartened many colonists; by July 1963, this pilot program had only 50 colonists left, approximately 250 of them having returned to their places of birth or sought out other colonies farther north in the Department of Santa Cruz.

In the colonization zone (La Enconada and El Campanario) to-

10. José Monje Rada and Roberto Vega, *Estudio de costos de colonización: comparación entre la colonización del Dpto. de Santa Cruz y el Alto Beni en el Dpto. de la Paz*, p. 37.

day, 80 colonists on 3,250 acres (including communal property) are cultivating an average of 10 acres, a few neither cultivating nor clearing any of their land despite available land-clearing equipment. Many grow sugarcane (a low average yield of 10 tons per acre), a source of cash income, only a part of which can be sold to the refineries due to a limiting quota system. The colonist grows corn on an average of 4.8 acres, sugarcane on 2.8 acres, rice on 1.3 acres, potatoes on 1 acre. Almost two-thirds of the colonists have been forced to seek work in off-the-farm occupations, since a critical 56 per cent of their land has already been cleared and is becoming increasingly unproductive,[11] or they turn to charcoal production both for home use and for sale.

In 1954, one year before the founding of the directed colonization effort at Cotoca, the colony of Aroma was established in an area of sandy loam soils with high scrub vegetation; this was a resettlement scheme for Cochabamba Valley farmers with partial assistance provided by a private or a governmental organization. Aroma began as the private plan of the brothers Eduardo and Oscar Arze, owners of large farms, to solve the valley's minifundia problem and to ascertain the adaptability of the Quechua-speaking *cochabambino* to the lowlands. The immediate need for agricultural development in an area highly geared to sugarcane production was, it is certain, not a small moving force in this plan.

Alternating groups of volunteers were first brought into this colony, twelve miles from Montero, in mid-1954 for two-month periods of work in road preparation, house construction, and partial deforestation of lots. After volunteering for three periods, anyone could apply for title to 38 acres; 14 colonists earned this right after a year, 29 by 1956[12] (the project now under CBF's auspices). First the Arzes, then CBF, provided free food for the first year plus some medical and technical assistance. Except for the awarding of plots by a CBF administrator stationed in Santa Cruz, and an on-location agricultural engineer, all direct help was terminated in 1959, and Aroma became (and still is) the site of *spontaneous* settlement by the colonist employable as jornalero on established plots until his soon-seeded land bore its first harvest. By 1960, over 200 families

11. Kelso L. Wessel, "Socio-Economic Comparison of Eight Agricultural Communities in the Oriente and the Altiplano," p. 64.
12. J. Colin Crossley, "Santa Cruz at the Cross-roads: A Study of Development in Eastern Bolivia," p. 233.

were located in the colony, yet "approximately 60 per cent of these colonists returned to their place of origin."[13]

Almost unanimously, the colonists turned to the *sindicato* (peasant league), which was organized primarily to acquire land bordering the settlement and which now constitutes the administrative center within Aroma. The first cooperative was created in 1961 with a membership of only 5 per cent of the colonists. Even today, the colonist, highly individualistic, scorns the work teams and credit responsibilities inherent in this arrangement. Instead, he may employ the traditional forms of mutual help evolved over the milennia by the Indians of the highlands.

Aroma today consists of approximately 240 families on 9,000 acres of land, an average of 20 acres cultivated per colonist. Sugarcane is emphasized (7.5 acres), for the colony is only 10 miles from the Guabirá sugar refinery; rice (5 acres) and corn (5 acres) are also important. However, Guabirá functions on a quota system so that only 64 tons of the colonist's annual crop of 150 tons reaches the refinery; the remainder is sold at low price on the open market in Santa Cruz or burned. Rice is sold on a rice-glutted market; low prices do not meet costs of hand production. And there is a lack of commercial alternatives for intensifying production of other crops. Hardly incentives for remaining in Aroma, yet seemingly preferred to the repayable debt incurred in directed colonies: "With everything, one concludes that, in spite of the problem of commercialization for the products of Aroma, the economic development of its colonizers exceeds the cost of installation of the colony, and, above all, the direct expenses per colonist. Besides, this experience shows that a colony already established and with possibilities of enlargement constitutes a source of attraction for many colonizers without direct governmental help."[14]

Two rather enterprising colonies were established in 1955 (Cuatro Ojitos) and 1956 (Huaytú) by the Bolivian Ministry of Defense, its objectives undertaken by the Army's Colonial Division. Four battalions "zeroed in" on the Santa Cruz area, clearing forest, cultivating land, and constructing roads, bridges, houses, schools, and wells. The soldier was to be offered fifty acres of land with a house upon completing his military service; unclaimed plots were prop-

13. Casto Ferragut, "Principal Characteristics of the Agricultural Colonies of Bolivia and Suggestions for a Colonization Policy," p. 130.
14. Monje Rada and Vega, *Estudio de costos de colonización*, p. 15.

agandized in the highlands and assigned to interested civilian colonizers in 1957—only after six months acclimatization by working in sugarcane harvests.

By 1958, this military colonization program was taken over by CBF, yet directed by army officials and 900 soldiers. And, by 1958, only 10 per cent of the conscripts had accepted plots; over 50 per cent of the personnel in Huaytú and Cuatro Ojitos were civilians from the highlands,[15] now settling spontaneously with some monetary help extended them by the military, none by CBF. Many also were leaving the colonies, disgusted with unfulfilled propaganda promises touted in the highlands. In 1961, CBF replaced the military with the Santa Cruz–based civilian administrator and the on-location agricultural engineer previously mentioned for Aroma. CBF-sponsored schools and health posts were provided.

Today, both exhibit some local administrative organization through popularly elected *consejos,* councils which administer special projects and coordinate group activities. With each colonist having 50 acres and averaging almost 15 acres under cultivation, Cuatro Ojitos, 55 miles from Santa Cruz, contains over 600 families on 43,000 acres of land; Huaytú, 75 miles from Santa Cruz, has approximately 170 families on 30,000 acres.

Again, sugarcane, rice, and corn are the principal crops. However, the farmer of Cuatro Ojitos has de-emphasized sugarcane so that many colonists have completely abandoned its production; the colonist who still produces it averages 5.8 acres in sugarcane, 5.5 in rice, and 1.5 in corn. The farmer of Huaytú refuses to become involved in the sensitive sugarcane market and averages 8.8 acres in rice and 5 in corn. In Cuatro Ojitos and in Huaytú, as in Aroma, both sugarcane and rice are victims of all the previously noted drawbacks to increased production. And in Huaytú, some of the plots already have been cleared of second growth, for "the colonists had, within an average of seven years, cleared 76 per cent of their land of its virgin forest,"[16] low-productivity land lying fallow only four to five years instead of the ten to fifteen years needed to rejuvenate the soil. Thus, an increase in off-the-farm employment, an increase in total abandonment.

Yet Bolivia's colonization plans are far reaching. A proposed

15. Crossley, "Santa Cruz at the Cross-roads," p. 232.
16. Wessel, "Eight Agricultural Communities," p. 22.

road between Santa Ana and Sararía-Mayaya will open some 27 square miles of land between the Alto Beni and Kaka rivers. Strips of land along both margins of the Alto Beni River northward from Santa Ana to the Inicua River and south to Covendo have been studied for potential colonization. In the Quiquibey River area toward Rurrenabaque, 180 square miles are mapped for the settler's ax, as are 5,400 square miles in the lowland plains of San Borja, Department of Beni. In this same department, the vast, scarcely populated watershed of the Mamoré River and its tributaries, Chipiriri, Isiboro, and Ichilo, is the subject of an extensive exploratory study as a zone for future development. In the Department of Santa Cruz, the area Yapacaní–Puerto Grether is being considered for further resettlement. In subtropical southeast Bolivia, the Abapó-Izozog region may realize its potential as an irrigation project, raising agricultural products and livestock for export; with current high yields of wheat and accessibility to the Santa Cruz–Yacuiba railroad, this sector eyes both domestic and international markets with hope.

Two German engineers recommended a grandiose Seven Years Rural Development Plan (1966–72), which presented coordinated power and land development features along the Rio Grande. Step 5 called for an independent colonization project based on upgrading some 350,000 acres of natural pasture lands to support thousands of beef cattle for the foreign market. Once this phase of the project was operational, the power and irrigation features would be pushed. Some half a million acres could then be valorized in the production of wet rice. This project had so many good features that it should be accorded more effort and capital investment than it will probably ever get, for it requires the pooling of skills and talents of many professions and a coordination of regional, governmental, and international efforts that has to date been extremely difficult to achieve.[17]

At the same time that the government has sponsored colonization operations in the Santa Cruz area, in Chaparé and in Alto Beni there has been much spontaneous migration completely lacking in government assistance.[18]

17. Bolivia, Ministerio de Economía Nacional, *Análisis econômico de los proyectos de colonización y de riegos*, pp. xix–xxi.
18. The valuable assistance of Mrs. Patricia C. Millet is gratefully acknowledged.

THE CHAPARÉ

It was in this tropical area of high precipitation at an elevation of 3,000 feet that the early Spaniards sought but failed to find easy wealth and that Franciscan fathers later established the Indian mission settlements of San Antonio (now Villa Tunari) in 1768 and Todos Santos in 1847. Throughout the late nineteenth and early twentieth centuries, *campesino* migration from the Cochabamba valley slowly spread into the Yungas to the east and onward into the Chaparé. The first national colony was created by the Decreto Supremo of October 2, 1920,[19] and was sited on the left bank of the Chaparé River near Todos Santos on an active regimental base of the Bolivian Army. The construction of a twenty-mile connecting road between Villa Tunari and Todos Santos, the initial planting of subsistence crops, the administration of the colony, were all duties of the army; by 1925, five hundred families had established themselves in the area.

The 1930 completion of the all-weather road, Cochabamba to Todos Santos, quickened spontaneous migration. There were 2,900 families by 1946. These *tolerados*, migrant squatters, took over and hacked out plots on state lands or on the furthermost corners of large private holdings. Chaparé expansion continued into undeveloped sectors when the Chaparé River suddenly changed course in 1947, engulfing homes and possessions. By 1966, the area embraced over fifty settlements (Todos Santos and Villa Tunari being the most important), totaling approximately 7,000 persons, primarily Quechuas from the Yungas of the Cochabamba area, families now having their rights protected by the government.

The colonists have cleared the land and built their homes without financial or technical assistance. Except for Army road-building efforts they have received no aid from the national government. Hence, they have turned to sindicatos, self-governing peasant leagues or local unions, to voice their demands. Administered by a secretary and a six-to-eight-man committee elected annually by and from its members, a sindicato collects a monthly tax from each colonist as well as a few days' labor for community projects (e.g., school construction and maintenance) and threatens expulsion for

19. Bolivia, Ministerio de Agricultura, Servicio Agrícola Interamericano, División de Ingeniería Agrícola, *"El Chaparé": capacidad agrológica y recursos naturales*, p. xvii.

the unheeding. The sindicato petitions the government for land and allots 25-acre parcels of land to the newcomer, who is promised legal title after residing on and farming the allotment for two years and clearing at least one-third of it. Yet, "at present, more than 90 percent of the colonists do NOT have such a title."[20]

Averaging ten acres under cultivation and producing commercially only plantains and rice, with some coca and citrus, the colonist of the Chaparé is hindered by lack of organized credit and technical aid in overcoming rudimentary agricultural practices and the resultant low productivity level. The one agricultural extension agent in the area can obviously offer only superficial support to the area's frustratingly slow development. However, the government's 1964 report, "El Chaparé": capacidad agrológica y recursos naturales, promises a new, if belated, look at this colonization zone; 268,000 acres have been made available for its sponsored Chimoré colonization project in this same area.

THE ALTO BENI

In the Department of La Paz, in the relatively steep slopes and fertile valleys of the Yungas of its heavily forested northeast sector, 105 miles from the nation's capital, the town of Caranavi lies at an altitude of 2,300 feet. It is the subtropical center of another area of voluntary and unassisted colonization. Yet forty-five miles beyond, after crossing an 8,200-foot pass, at the margins of the Río Alto Beni, is the community of Santa Ana de Huachi at 1,640 feet, hub of a Bolivia–United States directed pilot project, supported by the Alliance for Progress.

Interest in the area began with roaming Catholic missionary activity, the first mission being founded at the end of the seventeenth century; the mission center of Covendo on the Río Alto Beni was founded in 1842 and now serves 144 indigenous families.[21] A century of movement into the region was so accelerated, with the completion of the Coroico to Caranavi road in 1959 and the Caranavi to Santa Ana de Huachi road in 1961, that sixty spontaneous colonies, totaling over 2,200 families, were located in the Alto Beni by 1961[22] on lands of and delimited by the CBF. Many speak

20. Edelmann, "Colonization in Bolivia," p. 50.
21. Sánchez V. and Wessel, "Resumen de tres zonas de colonización," p. 6.
22. Ferragut, "Principal Characteristics of the Agricultural Colonies of Bolivia," Annex A.

both Spanish and Aymara, a few Aymara only. Many of them young and dissatisfied agriculturalists with small families, they came mainly from the Altiplano—a minority from the Department of La Paz' Yungas and metropolitan centers—without resources, without aid, a few to construct Altiplano homes of adobe walls and galvanized roofs, many to adopt the tropical wood-thatch home on 25-acre plots fronting 100 yards on the river or road.

Technical and credit assistance are, as in Chaparé, deficient. Only one agricultural extension agent serves the Caranavi settlers;[23] medical attention is available only in Caranavi or La Paz. Lacking the powerful and organized sindicato system of the Chaparé, the colonies are directed by a loosely structured administrative body of a Secretario General and a twelve-man committee elected annually by the colony from its members to keep the colony functioning, to handle matters dealing with the entrance of new colonists and with interior road construction, to administer tax funds, to construct schools, and to negotiate land titles. Land titles are to be obtained in two years if—an "if" rarely achieved—five acres are cleared and a dwelling constructed.

Those who do not work individually use traditional Altiplano cooperative arrangements, working with neighbors or friends, to overcome a scarcity of field hands due to small families, modest economic conditions, and the lack of cooperative organizations. The colonist averages only four acres under cultivation, mainly in rice and corn for subsistence, but produces, in addition, citrus fruits, coffee, bananas, and coca leaves for the market in La Paz, now only six hours away by truck.

Just beyond the Caranavi-centered zone of spontaneous colonization, halved by the Caranavi–Santa Ana de Huachi road, are situated the four nuclei, each planned for 120 to 150 families, of recent directed colonization. A fifth nucleus southeast of Santa Ana, fronting on the Río Alto Beni, completes this CBF–USAID planned and subsidized Alto Beni I project. The promulgation of a law of November 7, 1959, granting approximately 625,000 Beni Valley acres for immediate colonization, was followed by intensive on-the-

23. Antonio Murillo Christie, "Colonización de la zona Caranavi–Santa Ana de Huachi: estudio técnico socioeconómico," p. 30. Murillo Christie questioned 92 family heads in the spontaneous colonization zone on the differences between their present situations and their former residences, and recorded 80 (86.96 per cent) more and 1 (1.09 per cent) less pleased with the new location, 11 indifferent (11.95 per cent).

spot study and written reports by specialists in agriculture, public health, education, soils, geology, road-building, and air reconnaissance. In August 1961, pre-colonization efforts with 130 volunteer campesinos and a team of day laborers (jornaleros) opened 27 square miles of the area to well over 100 families in *each* of the five nuclei by 1963.

Under this dynamic colonization program, potential Bolivian colonists must meet five prerequisites: (1) preferably (not mandatory) at least two able-bodied family members between the ages of eighteen and forty-five; (2) previous experience in or aptitude for agricultural exploitation; (3) good health and no physical defects incompatible with agricultural tasks; (4) no criminal background; and (5) disposed to enter the colony with entire family and to sell land holdings in place of origin as soon as new undertaking proceeds satisfactorily.[24] It is hoped that a colonist will migrate in the company of friends and relatives from his own community or area.

The selection process is completed when one passes a medical examination and answers a questionnaire—determining, it is hoped, the colonist's intellectual capacity and degree of enthusiasm—on personal background, motives for migration, type of work acceptable, and additional help required in the colony. A contract, outlining his rights and obligations, is then signed by the accepted candidate. So much for on-paper requirements, those usually unfulfilled dreams of Latin American government planners. Who is actually entering this colonization area?

The Alto Beni I colonists, 90 per cent of the adult male population speaking Spanish and one or two indigenous languages (Aymara and/or Quechua), enter from the Altiplano (75 per cent), from the city (15 per cent), and from the Yungas (10 per cent). All decry the scarcity of available land, the further division of already small and "tired" plots, unemployment, and the lack of adequate communication routes. Married men comprise 75 per cent of the contract signers; 87 per cent of this total are accompanied by their families, which average 4.5 members. Almost one-half have agricultural backgrounds (some with knowledge of tropical agriculture); 39 per cent claim previous employment as city *obreros*; the remainder are merchants or miners. Literacy among family heads (almost all between sixteen and forty-nine years of age) is high (71

24. Corporación Boliviana de Fomento, *Reseña histórica del proyecto Alto Beni*, p. 30.

per cent), less so among wives (54 per cent) and children (36 per cent).[25]

Depending on soil quality, between twenty-five and thirty acres of land—three acres already cleared and planted in rice, corn, bananas, and yuca by the government—are provided the new colonist, three acres of which he must slash and burn annually to retain the title. On his arrival, the newcomer moves into a government-erected house, a makeshift dwelling which he must later replace by a more permanent one. He is also provided with tools, clothing, seeds, animals (two hens and a rooster), and medicine for the first year. During the first eight months of residence, he receives credit for the purchase of those foodstuffs not available on his planted three acres. This is no free-upon-request program, however. Of the total $2,500 invested per family,[26] approximately $600 (the cost of these supplies and services) must be repaid within fifteen years, payment commencing five years after settlement in the area. Educational, medical, and technical services are extended without charge.

The administrative setup links the project's main offices in La Paz to a Superintendencia de Obras in the colonization area where, in addition to administrators and staff, are located a hospital, an agricultural extension agent, a *mejoradora del hogar* (a kind of visiting home extension worker), and nurseries for the development of high-yield, diesease-resistant seedlings for the colonists. Immediate supervision and control is exercised by each Jefe del Núcleo, usually an agronomist, and his eight-man staff; a *sanitario* (public health agent), a teacher, and Peace Corps Volunteers add their support. There are popular Juntas de Mejoramiento Comunal which are encouraged by Bolivia's officialdom for two reasons: to work for the social, cultural, and economic improvement of the nuclei and to permit the use of colonist labor for several two-week periods annually to maintain schools, official buildings, sports fields, and so on. Yet only the first function has been carried out—and this primarily during the first two years of settlement. Although popular

25. Percentages based on Murillo Christie, "Colonización de la Zona Caranavi," pp. 44–53, from 90 interviews recorded throughout the Alto Beni I colonization zone. Asked how they viewed their present situation as compared to their former residence, Murillo Christie recorded 83 (92.22 per cent) more and 2 (2.22 per cent) less pleased with the new location, 5 (5.56 per cent) indifferent.

26. Bolivia, Secretaría Nacional de Planificación y Coordinación, Sector Colonización, *Plan bienal, 1965–1966*, p. 4.

support may be excellent, it is the support of the discontented, for settler mistrust of administrator finds voice in the local *junta*.

The colonist lives in a small settlement, *caserío*, of no more than twenty families whose long symmetrical lots parallel each other. Except for land designed "reserva forestal," caseríos are scattered throughout each nucleus, all having access to the 25-acre core of administrative offices, health post, school, and house for administrative personnel. The colonist averages six acres under cultivation, principally in rice (3.3 acres) and corn (1.5 acres). Coffee, cacao, citrus and bananas are also produced—currently on a small scale, yet with increasing government emphasis—as cash crops for both domestic and potential foreign markets.

Marketing has been a problem. The dirt road to La Paz is often impassable due to landslides and washouts; branch roads from colony to main road are often lacking. Only cacao can be marketed profitably, but transportation costs to La Paz are so prohibitive that the crop is flown to Covendo. There is unrest due to the pre-colonization charges for clearing and seeding three acres and for constructing slapdash houses—a debt which could be greatly decreased if the colonist performed these tasks himself. These pre-colonization promises are often completed *after* the colonist has been settled, often with his help. Experimentation with crops adaptable to the area has not provided an adequate agricultural base. Local topographic conditions add the problem of erosion on plots growing much-needed rice. Perhaps only citrus growing (for potential markets in northern Chile and southern Peru) and live-stock raising will be profitable.

Yet the colonists' adjustment to the Alto Beni and neighboring Caranavi area has been remarkable. "Only about 6 per cent of them do not make it and return home" (5 per cent are bachelors who find it impossible to succeed alone; 1 per cent are labor leaders who have failed to organize unions among the colonists).[27]

In 1964, the Corporación Boliviana de Fomento and the Banco Interamericano de Desarrollo inaugurated the Alto Beni II project, taking in Nucleus 5 of the Alto Beni I program, on some 54 square miles of virgin land along the Alto Beni River immediately south of Santa Ana. After undergoing the previously mentioned selection process and receiving financial and technical

27. Edelmann, "Colonization in Bolivia," p. 46.

assistance, without the local precolonization efforts and charges involved in the Alto Beni I program, the first colonists arrived in June 1964. Their backgrounds were rather evenly divided among agriculturalists, laborers, and craftsmen.

This embryonic project is surprisingly energetic—a rare quality in previous colonization projects. Three schools, two with native Aymara-speaking instructors, are initiating parent-teacher organizations and are providing literacy classes and libraries for adults. The agronomists circulate among the 1,200 families and two mejoradoras del hogar offer the women weekly classes in sewing, child care, cooking, health measures, and literacy. A physician and three sanitarios also serve the project. Two nurseries distribute citrus and cacao seedlings to the colonist during his first year in the project.

Alto Beni II is unique in its rather "well-oiled" administrative functioning. Each *brecha* or neighborhood elects a representative who presides over local meetings and who passes on the expressed complaints and/or needs of the brecha to the central Jefe de la Zona, a postion that should be held by an individual sensitive to the needs of the settlers. A BID-organized cooperative structure features a Board of Directors—a president, his committee, and two representatives from each brecha, all elected by and from the colonists—although all important decisions are made by the BID-salaried agent of the cooperative. The cooperative, emphasizing cacao production, provides $500 loans earmarked for the purchase of fertilizers, insecticides, some farm machinery, and vehicles. The colonist must also repay the costs of transportation to the colony, food provided during the first year, agricultural supplies, and neighborhood road construction. This charge, plus the $500 loan, seems an excessive burden for the inexperienced newcomer, especially in the recently opened, problem-ridden Alto Beni region.

Foreign Colonies

The 1953 agrarian reform program encouraged the selective immigration of foreigners into agricultural communities through a series of freedom-granting decrees. The Decreto Supremo of March 1953 lured into the Santa Cruz area from Paraguay 50 Volga-German Mennonites in 1954, 50 Dutch-German Mennonite families (some 350 persons) in 1958, and an additional 54 Mennonite families in 1964. The decree guaranteed their religious freedom, exemp-

Large-scale logging in the Japanese colony of Yapacaní, Bolivia, an operation preliminary to the introduction of permanent, intensive agriculture.

A typical slash-and-burn operation just across the road from the Japanese colony. Soil and timber resources are prodigally used up and the farmer clears another plot in a few years.

tion from military service, right to support religious schools, and right to obtain government loans. By 1972, some 500 Mennonite families had settled in the area seeking better lands and escape from a secular trend in community religion and education. A 1956 agreement between the governments of Japan and Bolivia, optimistically providing for the entry of 1,000 to 6,000 Japanese families into Bolivia, foreshadowed the peopling of the colony of San Juan with 16 families in 1957; the community had grown to 256 families by 1965. A similar agreement among the governments of the United States, Okinawa, and Bolivia in the early 1950s facilitated the resettlement of some 245 Okinawan families during the first year of colonization; by 1965, three centers contained 515 Okinawan families.

Both the Japanese colony of San Juan and the Okinawan settlements are administered as cooperatives of all residents with decision-making embodied in its popularly elected governing board and with its capital shared equally by the members of this communal farm. The Mennonites, instead, with individual ownership of land, annually select a member to act as salaried administrator, and each member is obligated to contribute a part of his year's labor to work on community projects. All equipment, as well as one's labor, is privately owned and rented to other Mennonite settlers at a fixed rate. Professional advice on agriculture, educational facilities, and medical care is available in all foreign colonies.

With 125 acres of land conceded to each colonist, the foreign colonies of Japanese and Okinawans concentrate on the commercial production of rice, and in 1965 averaged, respectively, 14 and 15.8 acres in rice per family (total acres under cultivation averaged 25 in both). There is also increasing emphasis on livestock; corn production for the fattening of pigs, which are sold locally as pork, averaged an additional two acres in San Juan and five acres in the Okinawan settlements.[28] Rice hullers, corn-huskers, and tractors, which are financed through entrance fees, are available to the communities. Each Okinawan colonist, working his own lands, can opt for having the cooperative market his crops at a 3 per cent tax on their market value; in San Juan the colonist is obligated to utilize the cooperative, also at a 3 per cent tax on the market value of his crops.

28. Monje Rada and Vega, *Estudio de costos de colonización*, p. 66.

The Mennonites are strongly isolationist, yet market-oriented (the men often speak Spanish while demanding that only German be used in the schools). The first group of Mennonites to arrive contracted to produce cotton when they bought 1,500 acres of land through the Compañía Algodonera Boliviana, a Santa Cruz textile firm. Two succeeding years of crop destruction by severe rains reduced the emphasis on cotton. On his 75–125 acres of land, averaging 8.8 acres in cotton, a colonist's cash crops now also include corn (23.8 acres), castor beans (5.5 acres), and peanuts (3 acres).[29] Twenty-three acres are used for improved pastureland, for large investment in livestock provides, as it has traditionally, a major source of Mennonite income. Yuca is grown for both hog and human consumption. Garden vegetables and fruit provide food for home use.

OVERVIEW

It is obvious that migration and resettlement in eastern Bolivia—and perhaps anywhere else—cannot be viewed as isolated phenomena; settlers and colonists are part of the warp and woof of an emerging cultural landscape. Transportation and marketing systems, universal education and public health measures, facilities for cheap and readily available credit for farmers, all are important and should be made available at the same time. If a settler has no credit, he cannot obtain seed; if he knows nothing of soils, he may clear and plant a plot on which little will grow; if there is no road or trail, he cannot market his produce—indeed he may find that there *is* no market for anything he *can* produce; and if he gets to the market and cannot speak the language of the people there, he may be robbed. These are the factors that form the cement of any society—particularly a society in an expanding, peripheral area—and the lack of any one of these, or other significant items, may put a very low ceiling on agricultural production, hence on the hopes and aspirations of the people in a pioneer zone. As documented in this chapter, many of Bolivia's colonists achieve only a scant increase in the level of living over what they enjoyed in their place of origin.

One of the most difficult tasks is to convince the peasant, the campesino, that all those interested in his resettlement, from neigh-

29. Kelso L. Wessel and Judith A. Wessel, "The Mennonites in Bolivia—An Historical and Present Social-Economic Evaluation," p. 31.

bors to public officials, are genuinely concerned for his betterment. This has certainly not been the case before, particularly with regard to public officials, and he must further be convinced of the worth of specific changes. To be sure, the highland campesino was highly motivated to change his diet from quinoa and potatoes to rice and corn: there was no other alternative if he planned to remain in the lowlands at all. In this case the reason for the shift in dietary habits was clear for him to see; to get him to change eating habits for the purpose of achieving a "balanced diet," or "proper caloric intake," or other nutritional desideratum, might be a very difficult task indeed. To get the campesino to fight stomach disorders by drinking boiled water is an even more difficult task, though one that can be achieved, particularly by intensive radio campaigns. Such campaigns have proved their worth in many of the more remote sectors of Latin America and could profitably be used in this area.

The peasant syndicates, an outgrowth of the 1952 revolution, achieved their original objective of acting as counterweight against vested landed interests and gradually came to exercise considerable political power. But the peasant leaders seemed uninterested in forming new agricultural cooperatives and have not even supported those agricultural cooperatives that have been established, except to try to exert control over them for political ends. Lack of funds, lack of education in cooperative methods, even dishonesty in the management of funds, have all aided in discrediting the cooperative movement in much of the Bolivian Oriente. A certain amount of success has been achieved by cooperatives in recently settled zones of the Yungas, due largely to the fact that membership in them is not compulsory and leaders are elected by members from among their own number, many of whom came from Altiplano communities bound together by ties of kinship and friendship.

Thus, by 1966, approximately 3,700 families had trekked eastward and resettled in the Bolivian lowlands through sponsored programs, and 16,000 families had settled spontaneously. The three colonies of foreign families added another 860, to total around 20,000 families (perhaps 80,000 people) resettled during the previous decade. Yet during this period, highland population multiplied by more than half a million. If the past witnessed little alleviation in highland population pressure, the future promises even less. Current CBF–BID programs promise the resettlement of 8,000 families (1,500 in the Alto Beni zone, 4,000 in the Chaparé-Chimoré zone, 2,500 in the Yapacaní zone) over a ten-year period at a cost of $9 million—less than one-fourth the *annual* population increase in Bolivia's three most densely populated departments![30]

Whereas Bolivia's recent self-sufficiency in sugar production is due to large farms, self-sufficiency in the dietary mainstay of the lowlands, rice, can be attributed to the nation's colonization programs, for most of the rice crop is produced by colonists in the Chaparé, Alto Beni, and Santa Cruz colonization zones. Increased corn production is also an accomplishment of the programs, which point to lowland family output as 2.7 times that in the highlands.[31] Yet economic gains are not so enticing as to precipitate a surge of highland-to-lowland migration, and sponsored projects fail for just this reason—the attraction, soon dampened, of immediate gain rather than interest in working at, and then proudly displaying, a new way of life.

The problems are many. Middlemen exploiting the subsistence farmer, especially during the harvests when cash is desperately needed, are the rule in the colonization zones. Transportation connecting production areas with highland markets is slow and costly. Technical assistance is needed, more so in directed colonies where the colonist is suddenly required to function in a strange environment among new neighbors, less so in spontaneous colonies where the colonist works for and learns from already settled friends and relatives before obtaining land on his own. There is a lack of adequate land for the entrepreneur who was stifled by limited land in the highlands. Many of eastern Bolivia's potential colonists are lost to the sugar mills of Argentina that pay their laborers' fares; many thousands have taken up permanent residence in that country, moving on to the cities after the six-month cane harvest. The Santa Cruz sugar mills offer no such inducements.

Foreign colonists, however—Japanese, Okinawans, and Mennonites—for whom capital is available, average almost four times as many acres per settler in rice and corn, the production of which is almost five times that of the Bolivian colonists. Although cotton is now the main money crop of the Mennonites, they are also increasingly emphasizing dairy products, and, when combined with swine

30. Kelso L. Wessel, "An Economic Assessment of Pioneer Settlement in the Bolivian Lowlands," p. 200.
31. Ibid., p. 202.

production, it is evident that both these activities will soon be controlled by foreign colonists.

The highways and railroads that converge on Santa Cruz, on an area better suited to commercial than to subsistence agriculture, have been powerful factors in the rapid economic development in that area: in the sectors of general agriculture, in ranches with improved breeds of cattle, and in sugar and cotton industries. This infrastructure, frail as it was, made it easier to open up the major oil fields northwest of the town of Santa Cruz. No such infrastructure characterized the Alto Beni and Chaparé zones.

On the future development of the Alto Beni, Dozier concludes that "Once the roads leading into the project and those within it are made stable and viable, the Alto Beni's regional relationships with the minifundia-pressured Altiplano, on the one hand, and with marginal slopelands of recent spontaneous settlement about Caranavi, on the other, will appear more pertinent. At present, the latter half of the 75 kilometers between Caranavi and the Alto Beni is most difficult to traverse and time-consuming—on occasion even during the drier season. It is mainly for this reason, and not because of lack of appreciation for the Alto Beni's agricultural superiority, that there has been heretofore no substantial flow of colonists from the adjacent zone of spontaneous settlement. They are not willing to trade accessibility for increased production; they can at least get the small quantities of fruits they manage to produce on their sloping fields to the La Paz market. Once the better lands of the Alto Beni are incorporated within this viable network, there will be a logical desire for many settlers to move on toward the river and into the directed project."[32]

32. Craig L. Dozier, *Land Development and Colonization in Latin America: Case Studies of Peru, Bolivia, and Mexico*, pp. 129–30.

REFERENCES: BOLIVIA

Bolivia. Ministerio de Agricultura. *La colonización e inmigración en Bolivia: Leyes—Decretos Supremos y otras disposiciones legales.* La Paz, 1965.
———. Ministerio de Economía Nacional. *Análisis económico de los proyectos de colonización y de riegos.* Cochabamba, 1965.
———. Ministerio de Hacienda. Dirección General de Estadística. *Boletín estadístico 1964*, no. 90.
———. Secretaría Nacional de Planificación y Coordinación. Sector Colonización. *Plan bienal, 1965–1966.* La Paz, n.d.

——. Servicio Agrícola Interamericano. División de Ingeniería Agrícola. *Capacidad agrológica de las tierras de colonización Santa Ana-Inicua*. La Paz, 1964.

——. *"El Chaparé": capacidad agrológica y recursos naturales*. La Paz, 1964.

Canelas, Amado. *Bolivia: un caso de reforma agraria*. La Habana: Centro de Documentación sobre América Latina Juan ₣. Noyola, Casa de las Américas, 1967.

Chardón, Carlos E., and Leigh, Stephen. *Desarrollo de la industria azucarera en el Departamento de Santa Cruz: informe (con una introducción sobre sus proyecciones en el planeamiento de la economía nacional)*. La Paz, 1959.

Corporación Boliviana de Fomento. *Programa de colonización: informe inicial*. La Paz, n.d.

——. *Reseña histórica del proyecto Alto Beni*. La Paz, 1965.

Crist, Raymond E. "Bolivia—Land of Contrasts." *American Journal of Economics and Sociology* 5, no. 3 (April 1946):297–325.

——. "Bolivians Trek Eastward." *Américas* 15, no. 4 (April 1963):33–38.

——. "Indians of the Bolivian Altiplano." *Geographical Review* 54, no. 1 (1964): 112–13.

Crossley, J. Colin. "Santa Cruz at the Cross-roads: A Study of Development in Eastern Bolivia." *Tijdschrift voor Economische en Sociale Geografie* 52, nos. 8–9 (August–September 1961):197–206, 230–41.

Cusack, Patricia L. "The Evolution of Colonization in Bolivia." Graduate term paper, University of Florida, 1967 (typescript).

Denevan, William M. *The Aboriginal Cultural Geography of the Llanos de Mojos of Bolivia*. Ibero-Americana, no. 48. Berkeley: University of California Press, 1966.

——. "Additional Comments on the Earthworks of Mojos in Northeastern Bolivia." *American Antiquity* 28, no. 4 (April 1963):540–45.

——. "Cattle Ranching in the Mojos Savannas of Northeastern Bolivia." *Yearbook of the Association of Pacific Coast Geographers* 25 (1963):37–44.

Edelmann, Alexander T. "Colonization in Bolivia: Progress and Prospects." *Inter-American Economic Affairs* 20, no. 4 (Spring 1967):39–54.

Ferragut, Casto. "Principal Characteristics of the Agricultural Colonies of Bolivia and Suggestions for a Colonization Policy." Report of an Agricultural Officer of the FAO, Office of Institutions and Rural Services, Subdivision of Land Tenure and Colonization, La Paz, 1961.

Fifer, J. Valerie. "Bolivia's Pioneer Fringe." *Geographical Review* 57, no. 1, (January 1967):1–23.

Heath, Dwight B. "The Aymara Indians and Bolivia's Revolutions." *Inter-American Economic Affairs* 19, no. 4 (Spring 1966):31–40.

——. "Bolivia under Barrientos." *Current History* 53, no. 315 (November 1967): 275–82.

——. "Commercial Agriculture and Land Reform in the Bolivian Oriente." *Inter-American Economic Affairs* 13, no. 2 (Autumn 1959): 35–45.

——. "Land Reform in Bolivia." *Inter-American Economic Affairs* 12, no. 4 (Spring 1959):3–27.

——. "Land Tenure and Social Organization: An Ethnohistorical Study from the Bolivian Oriente." *Inter-American Economic Affairs* 13, no. 4 (Spring 1960):46–66.

——; Erasmus, Charles J.; and Buechler, Hans C. *Land Reform and Social Revolution in Bolivia*. Praeger Special Studies in International Economics and Development. New York: Frederick A. Praeger, 1969.

Leonard, Olen E. *Santa Cruz: A Socioeconomic Study of an Area in Bolivia*. U.S.

Department of Agriculture, Foreign Agriculture Report no. 31. Washington, 1948.

Monheim, Felix. *Junge Indianerkolonisation in den Tieflandern Ostboliviens.* Braunschweig: Georg Westermann, 1965.

Monje Rada, José, and Vega, Roberto. *Estudio de costos de colonización: comparación entre la colonización del Dpto. de Santa Cruz y el Alto Beni en el Dpto. de La Paz.* La Paz: United States Aid Mission to Bolivia, 1963.

Murillo Christie, Antonio. "Colonización de la zona Caranavi–Santa Ana de Huachi: estudio técnico socioeconómico." Thesis for the degree of Ingeniero Agrónomo, Facultad de Ciencias Agronómicas, Universidad Mayor de San Simón, Cochabamba, Bolivia, 1964.

Osborne, Harold. *Bolivia: A Land Divided.* 3d ed. London: Oxford University Press (issued under the auspices of the Royal Institute of International Affairs), 1964.

Patch, Richard W. "Bolivia: U.S. Assistance in a Revolutionary Setting." In *Social Change in Latin America Today: Its Implications for United States Policy.* New York: Harper and Brothers, for the Council on Foreign Relations, 1960.

————. *Bolivia's Developing Interior: A Tour of Planned and Spontaneous Colonization Efforts.* West Coast Series, vol. 9, no. 3. New York: American University Field Staff, n.d.

Plafker, George. "Observations on Archaeological Remains in Northeastern Bolivia." *American Antiquity* 28, no. 3 (January 1963):372–78.

Sanabria Fernández, Hernando. *En busca de Eldorado: la colonización del Oriente boliviano por los Cruceños.* Buenos Aires: Imprenta López, 1958.

————. *Ñuflo de Chaves: el caballero andante de la selva.* La Paz: Editorial Don Bosco, 1966.

Sánchez V., Francisco, and Wessel, Kelso L. "Resumen de tres zonas de colonización y comparación de la agricultura del Oriente con el Altiplano." Report of the Bolivia-Cornell Project, La Paz, 1966.

Sariola, Sakari. "A Colonization Experiment in Bolivia." *Rural Sociology* 25 (1960):77–90.

Vellard, Jean Albert. *Civilisations des Andes: évolution des populations du haut-plateau bolivien.* Paris: Gallimard, 1963.

Weeks, David. "Bolivia's Agricultural Frontier." *Geographical Review* 36, no. 4 (October 1946):546–67.

————. "Land Tenure in Bolivia." *Journal of Land and Public Utility Economics* 23, no. 3 (August 1947):321–36.

Wessel, Kelso L. "An Economic Assessment of Pioneer Settlement in the Bolivian Lowlands." Ph.D. dissertation, Cornell University, 1968.

————. "Social-Economic Comparison of Eight Agricultural Communities in the Oriente and the Altiplano." Report of the Andean Indian Community Research and Development Program, Department of Anthropology, Cornell University, 1966.

————, and Wessel, Judith A. "The Mennonites in Bolivia—An Historical and Present Social-Economic Evaluation." Mimeographed. Ithaca, N.Y.: Cornell University, 1967.

Zondag, Cornelius H. *The Bolivian Economy, 1952–65: The Revolution and Its Aftermath.* Praeger Special Studies in International Economics and Development. New York: Frederick A. Praeger, 1966.

7. Regional Overview

THE CHANCE for the humid tropics of South America to achieve broadbased economic take-off in the next decade will depend, to a great extent, on agricultural innovations. With few exceptions, neither latifundistas nor political leaders nor the modern industrial elite have given much thought to the basic needs of agriculture. But as the tropical lowlands of the Amazon and Orinoco basins are being penetrated by settlers, new high-yielding crops are being evolved and grown in old farming regions as well as in pioneer zones, for local use as well as for export to highly competitive markets.

Research in agriculture has made possible the development and incredibly swift adoption of new types of rice and corn that are capable of phenomenal increase in output under the most widely varying conditions of soil, temperature, and available sunlight. Higher yields and higher prices will mean more money to the farmers of these developing areas, which in turn will provide them with the incentive and the means to acquire new equipment and to adopt new technologies. And, because of the dominant role of agriculture in this sector, what is good for the farmer will be good for the rest of the population, since the man on the land will have more money to buy the industrial output of the man in the towns and cities.

CATTLE RANCHING IN TROPICAL RAIN FOREST

In general the reasons for turning tropical forest into cattle ranches have been economically sound, even if at times ecologically questionable.

However, the labor available to the entrepreneur is unskilled, suited to the task of felling trees and clearing brush, leaving a tangle of vines, logs, and stumps to be fired when dry. Subsistence crops of corn, yuca, beans, pumpkins, and so on, are produced for a year or two among the charred logs and stumps, for use of the workers' families. Any surplus is sold, if there is a market. Harvesting these crops leaves the soil receptive to the growth of aggressive grasses onto which the entrepreneur turns in a head or so of stock for every three or four acres. Very little supervisory labor force is necessary. The entrepreneur is the only one with the capital to hire the laborers and to acquire and market the stock. The world protein shortage has been an added inducement to stockmen to increase the size of their operations. Cattle on the hoof can be driven to market, so it has not been necessary in many instances even to build roads. At present they can be walked to the end of the bus or truck line, to the airstrip, or to the local market. Thus, this kind of operation, if the rancher intensively manages his pasture, is in many ways a rational way of valorizing remote, forest-covered hinterlands.[1]

The Minifundismo of the Machete

As long as the struggle against the jungle is on the low technological level of the machete, the *serrano* settler may find himself in a new *minifundismo* imposed by the selva instead of the old one resulting from centuries-old institutional walls. Further, insecurity of tenure and the importance to the patch agriculturalist of marketing firewood or charcoal with which to get his first cash act together to help perpetuate nomadic or slash-and-burn agriculture, the rotation of fields instead of crops.

As long as most of the selva near penetration roads remains in the hands of the privileged few who are disinclined to give the land value by their own work and investments, agricultural progress is bound to be minimal. Thus, on properties with no fixed boundaries, or clear titles, and so far from access roads as to make marketing the crop a major undertaking, annual crops such as corn, beans, rice, yuca, and pumpkins continue to be grown, instead of the ecologically and sometimes commercially more desirable permanent tree crops such as cacao, rubber, cashew, and castor beans.[2]

The late Professor Edgar Anderson pointed out in his classic work[3] that the seemingly chaotic, multistoried mixture of crops

1. Raymond E. Crist, "Cattle Ranching in the Tropical Rainforest."
2. For further information on this subject see Crist, "Tropical Subsistence Agriculture in Latin America: Some Neglected Aspects and Implications."
3. *Plants, Man, and Life* (Boston: Little, Brown, and Co., 1952).

found in the kitchen gardens of the highland Indians of Guatemala used both soil and solar energy to maximum advantage; further, harvests were spread throughout the year. In the humid tropics as well, the most successful cropping system ecologically might well be that which most nearly mirrors the organization of the natural tropical forest: corn, tomatoes, sweet potatoes, squash, and beans could be grown on the ground floor, with bananas, yuca, chili peppers, and cacao growing in the next storey; crops of tall trees such as avocado, coconut, mango, breadfruit, and pehibaya palm could be grown in the highest storey.

Mixed cropping, the conscious and deliberate cultivation of more than one type of plant in one field at the same time, has many socioeconomic merits. The mixed crop field contains many different kinds of food plants grown simultaneously rather than in sequence; hence, it approximates the natural ecosystem of the tropical rain forest, being a kind of forest in miniature with its characteristic species diversity. The juxtaposition of many different kinds of plants in the same field or plot tends to minimize the incidence of pests and diseases. It makes possible harvestable food (e.g., cassava, yams, corn, beans) at any time throughout the year, and it prevents large seasonal fluctuations in the demand for labor. Ecologically, then, there is no alternative superior to mixed cropping. Research carried out in many parts of Africa reveals that, economically, intercropping gave higher cash returns per acre than pure stands. As Latin Americans continue economic development of the humid tropics, they should become more acutely aware of the diversity, the authenticity, and the intrinsic worth of their own autochthonous cultural and technical heritage, particularly of cultivation systems that took countless generations to refine. The more they experiment with such systems, the less likely they will be to slavishly follow models of large-scale, middle latitude, one-crop farming. More research on mixed cropping would certainly pay high returns, for it might prove that system to be the solution to many agricultural problems in the humid tropics.[4]

But long-range, intensive land management practices of this kind in the humid tropics are perhaps in most cases for the future. The small plot farmer has more immediate problems.

4. Matthias U. Igbozurike, "Ecological Balance in Tropical Agriculture," *Geographical Review* (October 1971) , pp. 519–29.

THE MANY FACETS OF LAND REFORM

Land reform should make land available to the settler, but it should also effect the modification of the rural power structure as an absolute prerequisite for rapid growth. Changes should be contemplated in the relations which farmers and farm workers have with each other or with nonfarm people, with respect to the land on which they live and work, with respect to its produce, and to the use of farm inputs and outputs.

In many instances the landlord has an extremely high bargaining power: perhaps he can effectively tie his workers to his property by extending "credit" at an interest rate of more than 100 per cent, which makes the worker, given his meager salary, essentially a serf; or the worker may have to work "obligatory days," at no pay, or at less than the prevailing wage rates; or a tenant may have to mine the land with soil-depleting crops, the cultivation of which speeds the process of erosion, in order to pay off an exorbitant rent; or the rural worker may be allowed to clear virgin land and live on it for two to five (or more) years, thereby greatly improving its capital value, only to be dispossessed from one day to the next with little or no compensation for his time, effort, and money invested. In any case, the man on the land has little motivation to increase production. In a society where such conditions exist, maximum use of the potential producing ability of the rural workers, or of the land, can hardly be expected, nor can the requirements of an industrializing economy based on rapidly increasing markets be met, nor can social and political balance be achieved. What John Kenneth Galbraith said in *The New Industrial Society* may still be true, that the imperatives of technology and organization, not the images of ideology, are what largely determine the shape and orientation of economic society. However, intangible factors are still operative in all societies.

The influence of incentive on productive capacity is seen in the U.S.S.R., where each worker on a Soviet *kolkhoz*, or collective farm, is allowed to have a small private plot of land on which he grows subsistence crops as well as perishable foods for sale in local markets. According to reports, 30 million of these tiny plots in the Soviet nearly half of all livestock products. These plots constitute only 3 per cent of the total area in crops in the Soviet Union, and the Union produce about 16 per cent of the total crop output and workers responsible for this high productivity on their private plots invest only a third of their labor on them. As the Spanish proverb has it, "the eye of the owner makes the horse fat." The private incentive of the workers on these small plots makes their labor inputs so efficient that productivity per unit area of this land is much greater than on the vast collectively worked sectors.[5]

The daily life of many primitive farmers is taken up with propitiating the gods, or trying to, or wishing one could propitiate them. The evil eye is a constant menace; every wind, every heavy rain, every drought, every phase of the moon—in short, every natural force—has its religious significance and must be interpreted. Every act is portentous, and, although the individual's disciplined, hemmed-about, and inhibited life might seem to him fulfilled, the fact is inescapable that his productive capacity and potential are, in the modern sense and to say the least, not at their maximum. These factors are mentioned merely to emphasize that what is true of the world's better developed lands is equally true of the hand-to-mouth agriculturalist of the less developed areas, namely, that increased production everywhere in the world is often a consequence of the motivations, attitudes, and capabilities of its people, rather than a consequence of material factors.

The average small-scale subsistence farmer does not think in terms of producing a surplus for the market, and, even if he should, the road or river tends to be a one-way street—the products that move over them tend to lose most of their value en route, as they must pay high transportation costs, or high taxes, or suffer outright confiscation at the hands of one who claims to own the land on which the produce was grown. Further, native peoples, ignorant of the official language, who occasionally try to enter the market economy are frequently, and sometimes even openly and flagrantly, robbed by the small village shopkeepers who consider themselves civilized. As long as these things go on, it will be difficult to orient the subsistence farmer in the direction of producing for the market. Roads and rivers should be two-way streets along which produce flows to market to be exchanged for cash or goods of sufficient value to make the trip worthwhile and to motivate further rewarding trips to that market on the part of the producer of raw materials.

5. D. Gale Johnson, "Soviet Agriculture," *Bulletin of the Atomic Scientist* 20, no. 1 (1964):8–12; quoted in Eric Wolf, *Peasants*, pp. 57–58.

The introduction of the outboard motor, particularly on dugout canoes, has greatly expanded the radius of action of the pioneer. (See p. 72.)

Although land reform usually begins with making land available to the settler, it should not end there. Laws that protect and broaden the rights of workers and producers will give them a modicum of economic power; the economically weak will achieve strength by forming cooperatives and by joining unions.

The police and courts should protect the rights, health, and safety of *all*, and resources should be made available to those who can use them to the greatest advantage. A *rational* program results when changes are induced in the rural power structure that make it economically successful. Some of these programs are technological in character, and most of them have political and social overtones: the small farmer and the rural worker would be greatly aided by broad resource studies, cadastral surveys, and clear titles to land; by education, housing, and sanitation; by cheap and easy short-term credit; by improved pricing mechanisms, and so on—the list is long indeed. We have in the past too often seen potentially useful citizens turned into paupers or outlaws. A rational agrarian reform reverses the process. It makes possible sedentary rather than shifting agriculture; it raises the farmer's productive capacity and his level of living, thus incorporating him into a cohesive, developing society —one in which he can now acquire a stake.

From Shifting to Permanent Agriculture

All the developing Andean countries under consideration have vast areas of virgin or unsettled land, a prime asset; this fact has the effect of encouraging wasteful, exploitative forms of agriculture—such as shifting agriculture even on fertile, level land—rather than more permanent cropping. However, as has been seen, changes are already underway. Pastoralism, mixed farming, and tree crops (bananas, palms, yuca, peppers) are successful in the savannas and riverside farms (*vegas*) of Venezuela and Bolivia and in the selva lands of Peru, Ecuador, and Colombia. In the study area there are thousands of small-scale pioneers who for the first time in their lives have their own land to farm. They have, for the most part, been successful in improving their levels of living. As more capital is available, the units of land in use tend to increase in size. This is a virtually universal phenomenon, whether the area under study be central Illinois or eastern Colombia.

Cattle ranchers in the Andean piedmont, eastern lowlands sectors of Colombia, Venezuela, Peru, and Bolivia, engage most successfully in extensive, nonmechanized land-use practices. They can walk their product to where it can be trucked or airlifted to Andean consuming markets. The large-scale sugar industry of eastern Bolivia continues to thrive. Even where rice is grown on a small scale by numerous farmers, production usually expands in response to the erection of a mill where it can be hulled, processed, and warehoused on a large scale, such as in Villavicencio, Colombia, in Barinas, Venezuela, and in Yurimaguas, Peru.

Important facets of the infrastructure, such as communications networks, public services facilities, and electric power plants, are being developed with national and/or international capital made available by the central governments. It is of strategic importance to these same central governments that the eastern Andean piedmont and tropical lowlands be tied to the centers of political power.

Good all-weather roads, assured markets, clear and secure titles to land, farms large enough to encourage innovation and mechanization, facilities for technical advice and rural credit—all are factors that draw the pre-industrial cultivator into the orbit of modernization and make him want to accept innovation and to refashion his own life. With these assured prerequisites a farmer, rather than hacking small plots out of the forest every few years, will be willing to clear, settle on, and improve one substantial piece of land, adequate for the support of himself and his family at a decent level of living. The most rapid progress is being made in those sectors that feature such an infrastructure with reasonably good highway connections to markets—Barinas, Venezuela; Villavicencio, Colombia; Tingo María, Peru; and Santa Cruz, Bolivia.

Yet the building of roads will not bring settlers; the Andean regional economies evolved without them. Roads were built when these economies had reached their limit of development, when a certain cultural frontier was reached. Factors and forces inherent in regional development—actual and potential—either exist or are latent. If these forces are not favorable in a new area, they cannot always be modified merely by building a road.

Making land available to peasants should go hand in hand with industrialization or other means of taking care of surplus rural populations. As a nation arrives at a higher stage of overall development, the role of the small farmer declines in importance—the number of those engaged in subsistence agriculture decreases, and thus automatically the problem of the small farmer becomes less acute. The Mexican Revolution has been successful to the extent that, not only has it made land available to the peasantry, but it has been able to forge a strong link between the political machinery of the national government and the peasant groups in the villages.

Major bureaucratic entities assume the task of dispensing patronage and thus achieve a tie between the state and the citizen that substitutes for the former old-fashioned personal relationship between patron and peasant, *hacendado* and serf. And with the new orientation goes a greater emphasis on large-scale, mechanized agriculture. Witness the high production of cotton, corn, and wheat on the government-controlled *ejidos* in many sectors of Mexico. Much the same result could be achieved by the Andean countries in their tropical sectors if their governments were willing to follow the example of Mexico by devoting comparable efforts and resources to making those areas productive.

But subsistence farmers in the colonization zones cannot introduce improved agriculture production such as the upgrading of livestock and research into pasture and range management; the protection of crops and livestock from pests and diseases; the rationalization of tools and equipment; the processing and marketing of produce. It is difficult to think of modernizing agriculture in a frontier zone without at the same time modernizing the entire cultural milieu, beginning with the society in the capital cities. It is perhaps more important and significant to achieve a new social and economic setting, in which the farmer can achieve lasting satisfaction for his moral and material aspirations, than to put improved methods of husbandry at his disposal.

General Bibliography

Bowman, Isaiah. *The Pioneer Fringe.* Special Publication 13. New York: American Geographical Society, 1931.

———. "Settlement by the Modern Pioneer." In *Geography in the Twentieth Century,* edited by Griffith Taylor. London: Methuen & Co., Ltd., 1957.

———, ed. *Limits of Land Settlement: A Report of Present-Day Possibilities.* New York: Council on Foreign Relations, 1937.

Butland, G. J. "Frontiers of Settlement in South America." *Revista Geográfica,* no. 65 (Dezembro 1966):93–108.

Castellanos, Juan de. *Elegías de varones ilustres de Indias.* Vol. I. Bogotá, 1959.

Chang, Jen-hu. "The Agricultural Potential of the Humid Tropics." *Geographical Review* 58, no. 3 (July 1968):333–61.

Crist, Raymond E. *Andean America: Some Aspects of Human Migration and Settlement.* Graduate Center for Latin American Studies, Vanderbilt University, Occasional Paper no. 3. Nashville: Vanderbilt University Press, 1964.

———. "Cattle Ranching in the Tropical Rainforest." *Scientific Monthly,* June 1943, pp. 521–27.

———. "Go East, Young Man." *Américas* 13, no. 6 (June 1961):3–9.

———. "The Indian in Andean America, I: From Encomienda to Hacienda." *American Journal of Economics and Sociology* 23, no. 2 (April 1964):131–43.

———. "The Indian in Andean America, II: The Basis for Development and Hemispheric Solidarity." *American Journal of Economics and Sociology* 23, no. 3 (July 1964):303–14.

———. "Politics and Geography: Some Aspects of Centrifugal and Centripetal Forces Operative in Andean America." *American Journal of Economics and Sociology* 25, no. 4 (October 1966):349–58.

———. "Tropical Subsistence Agriculture in Latin America: Some Neglected Aspects and Implications." In *Smithsonian Institution Report for 1963,* Publication 4586, pp. 503–19. Washington, 1964.

Denevan, William M. "A Cultural-Ecological View of the Former Aboriginal Settlement in the Amazon Basin." *Professional Geographer* 18, no. 6 (November 1966):346–51.

Dozier, Craig L. *Land Development and Colonization in Latin America: Case Studies of Peru, Bolivia, and Mexico.* Praeger Special Studies in International Economics and Development. New York: Frederick A. Praeger, 1969.

Eidt, Robert C. "Comparative Problems and Techniques in Tropical and Semi-tropical Pioneer Settlement: Colombia, Peru, Argentina." *Yearbook of the Association of Pacific Coast Geographers* 26 (1964):37–41.

Hanson, Earl Parker. "New Conquistadors in the Amazon Jungle." *Américas* 17, no. 9 (September 1965):1–8.

Hegen, Edmund Eduard. *Highways into the Upper Amazon Basin: Pioneer Lands in Southern Colombia, Ecuador, and Northern Peru.* Latin American Monographs, 2d ser., no. 2. Gainesville: University of Florida Press, 1966.

Hodder, B. W. *Economic Development in the Tropics.* A University Paperback Original. London: Methuen & Co., Ltd., 1968.

Holdridge, L. R. "Ecological Indications of the Need for a New Approach to Tropical Land Use." *Economic Botany* 13, no. 4 (October–December 1959): 271–80.

Meggers, Betty J., and Evans, Clifford, eds. *Aboriginal Cultural Development in Latin America: An Interpretive Review.* Smithsonian Miscellaneous Collections, vol. 146, no. 1. Washington: The Smithsonian Institution, 1963.

Phillips, John Frederick Vicars. *The Development of Agriculture and Forestry in the Tropics: Patterns, Problems, and Promise.* Rev. ed. New York: Frederick A. Praeger, 1967.

Platt, Raye R. "Opportunities for Agricultural Colonization in the Eastern Border Valleys of the Andes." In *Pioneer Settlement,* American Geographical Society Special Publication, no. 14, pp. 99–110 (1932).

Rouse, Irving. "The Intermediate Area, Amazonia, and the Caribbean Area." In *Courses toward Urban Life: Archeological Considerations of Some Cultural Alternates,* edited by Robert J. Braidwood and Gordon R. Willey. Chicago: Aldine Publishing Co., 1962.

Sauer, Carl O. *Agricultural Origins and Dispersals.* New York: American Geographical Society, 1952.

Snyder, David E. "The 'Carretera Marginal de la Selva': A Geographical Review and Appraisal." *Revista Geográfica,* no. 67 (Dezembro 1967):87–100.

Spinden, Herbert J. "La agricultura en la América pre-colombiana." *Cultura Venezolana* 12, no. 92 (1929):24–30.

Steward, Julian H., and Faron, Louis C. *Native Peoples of South America.* New York: McGraw-Hill Book Co., Inc., 1959.

Stewart, Norman R. "Some Problems in the Development of Agricultural Colonization in the Andean Oriente." *Professional Geographer* 20, no. 1 (January 1968):33–38.

Tosi, Joseph A., Jr., and Voertman, Robert F. "Some Environmental Factors in the Economic Development of the Tropics." *Economic Geography* 40, no. 3 (July 1964):189–205.

Turk, Kenneth L., and Crowder, Loy V., eds. *Rural Development in Tropical Latin America.* Ithaca, N.Y.: New York State College of Agriculture, Cornell University, 1967.

United Nations. *Demographic Yearbook, 1952.* New York, 1952.

Watters, R. F. *Shifting Cultivation in Latin America.* FAO Forestry Development Paper no. 17. Rome: Food and Agriculture Organization of the United Nations, 1971.

Webster, C. C., and Wilson, P. N. *Agriculture in the Tropics.* London: Longmans, 1966.

Wharton, Clifton R., Jr., ed. *Subsistence Agriculture and Economic Development.* Chicago: Aldine Publishing Co., 1969.

Wolf, Eric. *Peasants.* Englewood Cliffs, N.J.: Prentice-Hall, Inc., 1966.

Wolfe, Marshall. "Rural Settlement Patterns and Social Change in Latin America." *Latin American Research Review* 1, no. 2 (Spring 1966):5–50.

Wrigley, Gordon. *Tropical Agriculture: The Development of Production.* New York: Frederick A. Praeger, 1969.

Zavala, Silvio. "The Frontiers of Hispanic America." In *The Frontier in Perspective,* edited by Walker D. Wyman and Clifton B. Kroeber. Madison: University of Wisconsin Press, 1957.

Zelinsky, Wilbur. *A Prologue to Population Geography.* Englewood Cliffs, N.J.: Prentice-Hall, Inc., 1966.

UNIVERSITY OF FLORIDA MONOGRAPHS

Social Sciences

1. *The Whigs of Florida, 1845–1854,* by Herbert J. Doherty, Jr.

2. *Austrian Catholics and the Social Question, 1918–1933,* by Alfred Diamant

3. *The Siege of St. Augustine in 1702,* by Charles W. Arnade

4. *New Light on Early and Medieval Japanese Historiography,* by John A. Harrison

5. *The Swiss Press and Foreign Affairs in World War II,* by Frederick H. Hartmann

6. *The American Militia: Decade of Decision, 1789–1800,* by John K. Mahon

7. *The Foundation of Jacques Maritain's Political Philosophy,* by Hwa Yol Jung

8. *Latin American Population Studies,* by T. Lynn Smith

9. *Jacksonian Democracy on the Florida Frontier,* by Arthur W. Thompson

10. *Holman Versus Hughes: Extension of Australian Commonwealth Powers,* by Conrad Joyner

11. *Welfare Economics and Subsidy Programs,* by Milton Z. Kafoglis

12. *Tribune of the Slavophiles: Konstantin Aksakov,* by Edward Chmielewski

13. *City Managers in Politics: An Analysis of Manager Tenure and Termination,* by Gladys M. Kammerer, Charles D. Farris, John M. DeGrove, and Alfred B. Clubok

14. *Recent Southern Economic Development as Revealed by the Changing Structure of Employment,* by Edgar S. Dunn, Jr.

15. *Sea Power and Chilean Independence,* by Donald E. Worcester

16. *The Sherman Antitrust Act and Foreign Trade,* by Andre Simmons

17. *The Origins of Hamilton's Fiscal Policies,* by Donald F. Swanson

18. *Criminal Asylum in Anglo-Saxon Law,* by Charles H. Riggs, Jr.

19. *Colonia Barón Hirsch, A Jewish Agricultural Colony in Argentina,* by Morton D. Winsberg

20. *Time Deposits in Present-Day Commercial Banking,* by Lawrence L. Crum

21. *The Eastern Greenland Case in Historical Perspective,* by Oscar Svarlien

22. *Jacksonian Democracy and the Historians,* by Alfred A. Cave

23. *The Rise of the American Chemistry Profession, 1850–1900,* by Edward H. Beardsley